Introduct

Llandudno, known as the 'Queen of We between the impressive carboniferous li and Little Orme. Llandudno (meaning' after Tudno, a 6thC Christian who built the elegant town, largely built between 1849 and 1912 was purposely designed as a seaside resort, under the guidance of the wealthy Mostyn family. The arrival of the branch railway in 1858 ensured its development into the premier visitor destination it remains today. The Great Orme, which is now managed as a country park and nature reserve, is a Site of Special Scientific Interest, a Special Area of Conservation, and has Heritage Coast status. It contains cliffs which are home to a variety of sea birds, impressive crags, limestone pavements, grassland and heathland, roamed by its famous feral Kashmir goats. Running around its cliffs is a delightful Victorian toll road, and rising to its summit (679 feet/207 metres) is Britain's only cable-hauled road tramway – both engineering marvels. There are many sites of historical and archaeological interest, including extensive Bronze Age copper mines. From Llandudno the beautiful North Wales coast extends via other seaside resorts to Prestatyn. Together they offer stunning coastal scenery and views, best appreciated on foot.

The 30 walks in this book comprehensively explore the landscape and history of this part of the North Wales coast. They visit sites of historic interest including medieval castles, an Iron Age hillfort, a Neolithic burial chamber, ancient churches, manor houses and nature reserves. They feature low limestone hills, woodland, beaches, dunes, town trails, and river estuaries. They include five linear walks linked to local bus services following the new Wales Coast Path from Prestatyn to Conwy.

The routes, which range from a simple 1½ mile waymarked nature reserve trail to an 8½ mile section of the Wales Coast Path, are well within the capability of most people. Many routes contain shorter walk options. A key feature is that individual walks can easily be linked with others to provide longer day walks if required. They follow public rights of way or permissive paths. Walking boots are recommended, along with appropriate clothing to protect against the elements. Please remember that the condition of the paths can vary according to season and weather!

Each walk has a detailed map and description which enables the route to be followed without difficulty, but be aware that changes in detail can occur at any time. The location of each walk is shown on the back cover and a summary of the key characteristics of each is provided. This includes an estimated walking time, but allow more time to enjoy the scenery.

Please observe the country code and respect any ancient site visited. *Enjoy your walking!*

LLANDUDNO

DESCRIPTION A 4½ mile walk (**A**) exploring Llandudno and its history from prehistoric times, incorporating the town's best features and views, as well as key information boards on a designated Llandudno Town Trail (leaflet available from the Tourist Information Centre). The route starts in the heart of the Victorian resort, takes in a section of North Shore's majestic promenade and the 19thC iron pier, then rises through Happy Valley Gardens to visit an Iron Age hillfort. After descending through the Old Town area to the hillside Haulfre Gardens it follows the Invalids/ Lovers Walk across the open hillside. After a short stroll along West Shore, it returns along the northern edge of the Victorian resort. Allow about 3 hours. An alternative 3½ mile walk (**B**) omitting West Shore is included.
START Library/Tourist Information Centre, Mostyn Street, Llandudno [SH 783823].

*E*arly man *settled in the area during the Stone, Bronze and Iron Ages. By mid-19thC Llandudno was a small community of less than 1000 people engaged primarily in working on the land or in the Great Orme copper mines. In 1849 the Mostyn family, local wealthy landowners since the 16thC, revealed plans for a new town on recently enclosed land. Under their guidance in ensuing years the town was laid out in a grid pattern that curved to reflect the sweep of the bay, with wide streets and attractive buildings.*

I Walk south east along Mostyn Street – *the town's main shopping street and the heart of the new Victorian town, along which trams ran to Colwyn Bay from 1907 to 1956.* Shortly you pass Holy Trinity Church and information board 2. Continue to information board 4 at North Western Gardens – *an important urban open space with toilets.* Go over the Pelican Crossing and along Vaughan Street opposite to reach Mostyn Crescent. Go onto the promenade and after admiring the sweeping view towards the Little Orme, walk towards the Great Orme. *The wide promenade, built on a natural*

shingle bank, and the elegant hotels created a classical frontage to the new resort. Go past the former bandstand and information board 5, to reach information board 6 at the Cenotaph. Continue along the promenade to information board 7 which details the town's transport history, then follow the pier walkway behind the Grand Hotel (1901) and continue along the elegant iron structure to its end *The current pier was built in 1876/7 to replace an earlier one destroyed in 1859 by a storm. It was later extended to the promenade, making it the longest in Wales at 2,295 feet.* Return to go through its original gated entrance to information board 8 opposite, beneath the terminus of the cable car (1969). Walk along the pavement overlooking the rocky shore towards the eastern tip of the Great Orme.

2 Just before the castellated toll house at the start of Marine Drive – *a spectacular engineered route round the Great Orme's cliffs which opened in 1878* – cross the road and follow a part stepped path up the side of Happy Valley. *This former quarry was gifted by Lord Mostyn and landscaped into gardens to commemorate Queen Victoria's golden jubilee in 1887.* After climbing steadily up the edge of the terraced gardens, continue up the waymarked Summit Trail. Just before steps leading up to a waymarked wooden gate in the top right hand corner of the gardens, turn LEFT past a stone shelter. Cross the road to a wooden gate and follow a stepped path up to an information board on Pen Dinas, with the dry-ski slope and toboggan run (1986) nearby.

3 Go up steps, then take the path's waymarked left fork, which zig zags up the part wooded side of Pen Dinas. At a path junction turn LEFT up to its summit with an information board on its Iron Age hillfort and nearby 'Rocking Stone (Maen Sigl)' at a superb viewpoint. Return down to the path junction then descend to a lower path by the car park. Follow it to the nearby road. Turn LEFT down the road to crossroads by the tram line. Go up Llwynon Road opposite, then turn LEFT along Rofft Gate to a kissing gate. Follow the path along the wood edge

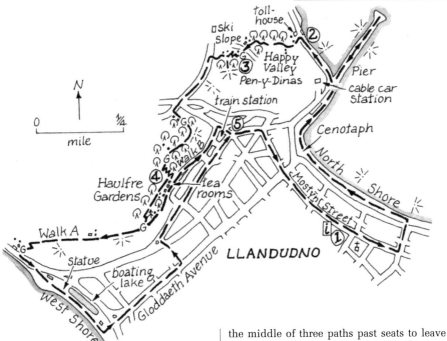

past a kissing gate giving access to a seat at a great viewpoint. Continue with the woodland path, past a waymarked 'Summit' side path. After a small gate descend the waymarked 'To Town' railed zig zag path to reach a path junction near the bottom.

4 Here you have a choice. (For **Walk B** continue along the wood edge, always on the higher railed path, shortly descending to go through an iron gate at the edge of Haulfre Gardens. After a short walk along the Invalids/ Lovers Walk to enjoy the extensive views return to the gate and follow the wide path through the Gardens past the Tea-Rooms to the entrance, with information board 12 to your right. Go down Cwlach Road and along the narrow road ahead (Llwynon Gardens) to reach Old Road with its tram line. Follow it down past the King's Head – *Old Llandudno's main hotel until 1850* – to reach crossroads and information board 11 just below the Tram Station, to join Walk A at point **5**.) For **Walk A** continue down the waymarked path to a narrow road and toilets in Haulfre Gardens. Follow the road past Haulfre Tea-rooms, then

the middle of three paths past seats to leave the Gardens by an iron gate. Follow the wide path, known as Invalids/Lovers Walk, across the open hillside – *enjoying extensive views* – later descending to the western end of Marine Drive by another toll house. Turn LEFT. Shortly go along the promenade at West Shore – *once an industrial area for sorting ore from Great Orme copper mine* – past the White Rabbit Statue (1933), then the model boating lake – *formed from an earlier pool being used about 1850 for washing crude copper ore.* Just past toilets turn LEFT past a children's play area, then go along the left-hand side of Gloddaeth Avenue – *a wide boulevard linking the North and West Shores.* Shortly, turn LEFT on a signposted path along Gloddaeth Way. Cross Abbey Road, then bear RIGHT along Church Walks until you reach the Tram Station. *The cable tram to the summit opened in 1902.*

5 Continue along Church Walks to information board 10 at a junction of 5 roads marking the boundary of the Old town and the Victorian resort. Go down Mostyn Street to a roundabout and on past information board 15 to the start.

3

WALK 2

ST TUDNO'S CHURCH

DESCRIPTION A 3¼ mile walk exploring the eastern section of the Great Orme. After climbing through Happy Valley Gardens, the route continues past an ancient well to 12thC St Tudno's church, then returns along Marine Drive, offering delightful coastal scenery (See Walk 7 for information.). Allow about 2 hours.
START Cenotaph, northern end of the North Shore Promenade, Llandudno [SH 782826].

I Walk to the front of the Grand Hotel, then take the road signposted to the ski slope, soon bending into Happy Valley. At the end of the cafeteria, take the pathway on the right, then follow the waymarked 'Summit Trail' as it winds its way up through the attractive terraced gardens to a wooden gate at its top right hand corner.

2 Go up the stepped path with the toboggan run and dry ski slope nearby. At the first bench seat take a path up on the right and onto the limestone hilltop to a superb viewpoint – *the pier, Little Orme, Llandudno, Deganwy, Conwy, and the Carneddau mountains.* Afterwards continue up the stepped path to its top.

3 At a finger post, follow the wide path ahead signposted to 'St Tudno's church' – *soon with a view of the Summit Complex and the church.* Follow the waymarked 'Summit Trail' path to a kissing gate and on past a farm to reach Ffynnon Powell. *Folklore says this spring miraculously appeared after a farmer named Powell and his family prayed for God's intervention at St Tudno's church during a time of severe drought, when they were refused access to the area's wells.* Soon you reach the road by St Tudno's church. The neat 12thC church was named after Tudno, a 6thC Christian who built the first church in the area, and was Llandudno's original parish church.

4 After visiting the church go down the road, then take a signposted path just beyond the bend, which meanders down to rejoin the road. Follow the road down to the junction with Marine Drive, which you then follow east. As you turn the corner, views across to the Little Orme appear, followed by the pier and the splendid frontage of Llandudno. *The limestone cliffs tower above you, alive with the sound of nesting birds. You pass a series of arches, formed by stone extraction.* Go past the toll house, the Happy Valley Gardens and on back to the start.

WALK 3

PEN DINAS

DESCRIPTION A 3 mile undulating walk (**A**) exploring part of the Great Orme's upland area, offering extensive views. From the summit (679 feet/207 metres) the walk follows a choice of routes down to the Halfway tramway station, then descends in stages to pass the Ski Centre, before visiting Pen Dinas Iron Age hillfort. It then returns to the summit by an ancient well and 12thC St Tudno's church. Allow about 2 hours. A 2¼ mile walk (**B**) omitting Pen Dinas is included. Another option is to take the cable car, tram or bus to the summit, follow the walk to Pen Dinas then return through Happy Valley Gardens, or continue to St Tudno's church and follow Walk 2's return via Marine Drive.
START Great Orme summit [SH 766853].
DIRECTIONS The summit can be reached by car, no. 73 bus, cable car and tram.

*T*he present Summit Complex was built as a hotel in 1903, and the surrounding area was developed as a golf course. The hotel was owned by Randolf Turpin, once world middleweight boxing champion. It is the terminus of Britain's most spectacular funicular tramway, which has operated since 1902, as well as Britain's longest aerial cabin lift, built in 1969. Nearby is a Visitor Centre. During the 19thC, a semaphore station, one of a chain built by Liverpool Dock Trustees, operated here, transmitting messages between Holyhead and Liverpool. From the trig point are panoramic views.

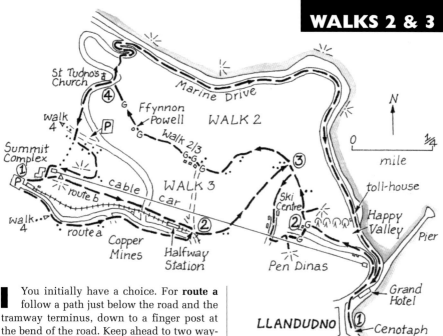

St Tudno's Church
Marine Drive
walk 4
Ffynnon Powell
WALK 2
Summit Complex
walk 2/3
WALK 3
cable car
Copper Mines
Halfway Station
Pen Dinas
Ski Centre
Happy Valley
Pier
toll-house
route b
route a
walk 4
N
0   ¼
mile
Grand Hotel
LLANDUDNO
Cenotaph

1 You initially have a choice. For **route a** follow a path just below the road and the tramway terminus, down to a finger post at the bend of the road. Keep ahead to two way-marked 'To Town' paths at a fence corner. Follow the one leading LEFT down past an information board, then angle LEFT on a path signposted to the Ski Centre. After crossing the road leading to the nearby Copper Mines, continue with a waymarked path beside the Summit access road. After passing the Half-Way tramway station you reach an information board just before a kissing gate. Here cross the road and tram line, just before the bend, then turn RIGHT. For **route b** from the trig point follow a path down towards the tram line then near it down to pass close behind the Half-Way station to reach a stony track. Keep ahead.

2 Go up the stony track past a barrier and continue with the wide waymarked path, past the cable car pillar then down towards the sea – *with the windfarm and Little Orme visible* – to reach a finger post at a path junction. (For **Walk B** follow the signposted path to St Tudno's church, then paragraph 4.)

3 Keep ahead for a few yards, then descend a stepped path to a waymark post. Here take a path on the right down the edge of the toboggan run and dry ski slope, then a track past the Alpine Lodge. Go down the road and at the car park entrance turn LEFT

along a path. Go up its right fork and follow the waymarked path to an information board on the summit of Pen Dinas. *This area is a Scheduled Ancient Monument containing many features of archaeological interest, and is the site of an Iron Age fort – with over 60 round houses. Beyond is the 'Rocking Stone (Maen Sigl)' at a superb viewpoint. The stone is reputed to have been used by druids in dealing with people accused of certain acts. The person stood on the stone, and only if it rocked, was he/she declared innocent!* Return down to the path junction, then follow the path RIGHT down to another information board by the road. Descend the stepped path to a gate, go across the road and past a stone shelter, then turn LEFT up steps to a wooden gate. (Now follow instructions in paragraphs 2 & 3 of **Walk 2** to St Tudno's church.)

4 After visiting the church continue up the road past the cemetery. Shortly take the waymarked Summit Path across open ground and over a stony track. At the next cross-road of paths you have a choice of routes to the summit. Instead of the direct steep route, turn LEFT over crosspaths, then follow the waymarked path up past an information board to the Summit Complex.

WALK 4

THE GREAT ORME (WEST)

DESCRIPTION A 6½ mile walk (**A**) exploring the western half of the Great Orme, full of interest, with superb coastal and limestone scenery, and panoramic views. The route follows a path beneath cliffs, then the scenic Marine Drive up to pass Pen-y-Gogarth (Great Orme's Head), with its former cliff-top lighthouse and café. Later the walk heads inland up past 12thC St. Tudno's church to just below the summit. It then meanders around delightful upland limestone country, past an ancient well, to the south side of the summit. It continues past the Copper Mines to a Neolithic burial chamber, then makes a stunning descent to finish on a popular Victorian hillside promenade. Allow about 4 hours. The route offers an alternative finish by the Monk's Path, making for a 5½ mile walk (**B**) and a shorter 5 mile walk (**C**) taking in the summit with its Visitor Centre and café.

START Boating lake, West Shore promenade, Llandudno [SH 771821] Alternatively the Summit car park [SH 766853].

DIRECTIONS The boating lake lies at the northern end of West Shore promenade. Plenty of roadside parking is available.

West Shore was once an industrial area for sorting ore from the Great Orme copper mine. The ore was washed in a pool here in the mid-19thC, which was later developed into the model boating lake. The nearby 'White Rabbit' statue was erected in 1933 to promote the town's association with Alice Liddell, the inspiration for Lewis Carrol's Alice in Wonderland, who reputedly spent several summers nearby with her family from 1861.

I Walk north along the promenade and continue along Marine Drive, then go through a kissing gate on the right near the castellated stone toll house. Just beyond turn LEFT up a path and follow it beneath eroded cliffs – *enjoying a stunning view across the bay* – to eventually reach a lane by houses.

Follow it to rejoin Marine Drive. The scenic road rises steadily beneath limestone buttresses, offering great seaward views. *Folklore has it that the sea hides the legendary lands of Helig which disappeared under the waters in the 6thC. Later, you will see below the Gunsite – an important Second World War military training area (See Walk 6).* The road then bends towards Pen-y-Gogarth (Great Orme's Head), soon passing Ffynnon Gaseg (Mare's Well) – *which once serviced the passing horse-drawn traffic.*

2 Just before the next bend a waymarked Nature Trail path gives good views of the high cliffs. Continue along the road, past the Rest & Be Thankful Café, then the entrance to The Great Orme's Head Lighthouse. *This castellated two- storey building, designed by the Chief Engineer of the Mersey Docks and Harbour Board and set high on the steep cliffs, served as a lighthouse from 1862 until 1985, after which it became a unique bed and breakfast establishment. It said to be haunted by the ghost of Austin, a former lighthouse keeper, who drowned trying to save a mariner.* The road now steadily descends through the dramatic landscape of limestone crags and steep cliffs with their many seabirds, later levelling out – *with a good view back to the lighthouse.* At a road junction do a sharp U-turn RIGHT up the zig-zag side road. Shortly, take a signposted path, keeping to its right fork, up to rejoin the road by St. Tudno's church. *This neat 12thC church was named after Tudno, a 6thC Christian who built the first church in the area, and after whom Llandudno (meaning' enclosure' of Tudno) was named.* Follow the road past the churchyard, then take the waymarked Summit path across open ground to reach a stony track. (For **Walk C** follow a choice of paths up to the summit. Head down to the Visitor Centre/Tramway terminus, then follow a path down below the road to a finger post on the bend. Keep ahead to point **4**.)

3 Follow the track RIGHT across the hillside past an information board, then Ffynnon Rhufeinig (*the Roman Well – although its connection with the Romans is uncertain*) to a gate. Continue along a wide

Pen-y-Gogarth

Great Orme's Head
lighthouse

café

Ffynnon Gaseg

limestone pavements

Ffynnon Rufeinig

summit complex

walk 2

St Tudno's

walk 2

copper mines

walk 3

Marine Drive

walk B

walk C

P

quarry

cromlech

West Shore

LLANDUDNO

lake

N

0 ¼ mile

path, following the wall across a delightful limestone plateau, featuring occasional large glacial erratic boulders. Later the wall bends left, and after passing limestone pavements and gorse, rises to a small stone cairn at a superb viewpoint. Continue beside the wall, shortly reaching a waymark post. (For **Walk B** go to another post to your right, marking the start of Monk's Path, which descends to Marine Drive. Follow it back to the start.) Continue beside the wall then at its corner by an information board follow a path angling LEFT up the slope and on past Bishop's Quarry to a finger post by the bend of the road. Angle RIGHT.

4 At the nearby fence corner there are two waymarked 'To Town' paths. Follow the one leading LEFT down past an information board and finger post to a road at the entrance to the Copper Mines – *whose earliest workings date from the Bronze Age, some 4,000 years ago. It is believed to be the most extensive copper mine of the ancient world.* Turn RIGHT past the gated entrance to a house and follow a track past the entrance to Pen-y-Gogarth Nature Reserve, then mine buildings, through a gate and on past houses. Keep ahead along Pyllau Road. At a junction, turn RIGHT, then RIGHT along Cromlech Road to view the Cromlech – *a Neolithic Burial*

Chamber, dating from 3,500–2,500 BC, known as Llety'r Filiast (the hair of the greyhound bitch). Return to the junction and turn RIGHT along the road.

5 At the wall corner of Baron Hill, turn LEFT down past a converted chapel, then descend an initially stepped path to a road by a junction. Turn RIGHT along Tyn-y-Coed road. Follow it past houses to its end by Anglesea Road at a fine viewpoint. Go through a kissing gate and take a path angling RIGHT across the open hillside. After about 50 yards, descend a waymarked stepped path on the left, soon zig-zagging down the steep open hillside – *enjoying panoramic views* – to a tarmaced path by a stone shelter – *known as the Invalids/Lovers Walk.* Follow it RIGHT, later descending to join your outward route.

WALK 5

MAES-Y-FACRELL

DESCRIPTION A 3 mile walk (**A**) exploring the Great Orme's summit, featuring the open slopes of Maes-y-facrell, limestone pavements, ancient well and panoramic views. Allow about 2 hours. An alternative 2½ mile walk (**B**) is included.

START Great Orme summit car park [SH 766833].

DIRECTIONS The summit can be reached by car, no. 73 bus, cable car and tram.

1 At the western end of the car park go onto higher ground for views to the tip of the Great Orme. At the facing fence turn LEFT down a path, soon bending LEFT and passing beneath the car park to a gap in the wall/fence corner. [For **Walk B** turn right and descend a path to the wall corner at point **2**.] Angle LEFT to a finger post by the road and tram terminus, then follow the wide path just below the road down to another finger post on its bend. Keep ahead to two waymarked 'To Town' paths at a fence corner. Continue ahead along a narrow old green track on to Maes-y-facrell, then turn LEFT along the wide waymarked path to reach a superb viewpoint – *looking south to Conwy castle and the Carneddau mountains, and east to the Little Orme and Rhyl.* Descend to the next waymark post, then turn RIGHT along a path across the hillside, soon bending north west past side paths. The delightful wide path then descends – *with a view of the Summit Complex* – to a wall corner by an information board.

2 Keep ahead, then take the left fork and follow the wide path along the edge of the steep hillside. Shortly rejoin the other path by the wall, soon rising steadily past waymark posts to a small low stone cairn. Continue down beside the wall, then just beyond old iron gates take a path angling away from the wall. Soon at a crossroad of paths, take the right fork, and at a nearby path junction keep ahead past a limestone pavement. At the next junction keep ahead with the wide path past another limestone pavement. At another path junction bear RIGHT along the wide path.

3 At a crossroad of paths opposite the nearby wall corner, keep ahead, soon passing erratic glacial stones to reach waymark post 7. Follow the path down to join a wider path by the wall. After a gate continue along a track, past Ffynnon Rhufeinig (Roman Well) and an information board, then a view overlooking St Tudno's church. About 40 yards after the gated entrance to a cottage take a path on the right angling up the hillside towards the summit. After passing beneath the cottage take the path's right fork, past the wall corner and up to a higher wall/fence corner. Follow the path up to a green cross-track, then another path opposite up to pass between the cable car terminus and the Summit Complex.

WALK 6

GUNSITE

DESCRIPTION A 4¾ mile (**A**) or 4 mile (**B**) walk exploring the Great Orme's western tip, offering panoramic views. From Marine Drive the route follows Monk's Path up onto the headland, then explores the limestone edges before descending to the Gunsite which played an important role in the Second World War. A path beneath limestone crags makes a spectacular finish. Allow about 3 hours. A lower level alternative 3 mile walk (**C**) to the Gunsite is included.

START Boating lake, West Shore promenade, Llandudno [SH 771821].

DIRECTIONS The lake lies at the northern end of West Shore promenade. Plenty of roadside parking is available.

On a shelf beneath Marine Drive is an area known as the Gunsite, where the Royal Artillery ran Officer Cadet courses in gunnery, wireless and searchlight skills from 1941. From 1942-44 the Coast Training Regiment was based here. At its peak in 1942, this peaceful green coastal site, now managed by Conwy Countryside Service, housed 745 people of various ranks and ran up to 14 courses. Little now remains of this once important and bustling wartime facility. For information on West Shore see Walk 4.

Great Orme's Head

cafe

Ffynnon Gaseg

area of limestone pavements

WALK 6

WALK 5

Ffynnon Rhufeinig

cairn

Gunsite

WALK 6

Marine Drive

Walk B

summit

quarry

Maes-y-facrell

N

0 — ¼ mile

West Shore

boating lake

low a path along the top of the cliffs, passing another limestone pavement. When the Summit Complex comes into view the path bends towards it. At a crossroad of paths turn RIGHT and follow the path past the nearby large boulder, then to the right of another squat boulder, known as 'The Hamburger'. Soon the path bends LEFT and climbs onto higher ground ahead. When it splits keep ahead to the highest point, then follow a path LEFT past a short old embedded iron post back to the concrete road at point **2**.

1 Walk north along the promenade to join Marine Drive. Continue along the pavement – *enjoying views across to Anglesey and the Carneddau mountains* – passing beneath the western crags of the Great Orme to where the road splits. (For **Walk C** go along Llys Helig Drive, explore the Gunsite, then follow the main walk's return.) Continue along Marine Drive to an information board, then take a signposted path opposite. Monk's Path – *reputedly used by monks in the past* – rises steadily across the steep hillside to a waymark post at the top – *with a view of the Summit Complex*. Keep ahead to join the nearby wall. Shortly you reach a small low stone cairn. Here angle LEFT to join a nearby wide path heading north, soon descending and continuing past a nearby car park. The path then bends down past waymark post 5 by a fenced off limestone pavement. Go past a post and along the edge of a picnic area to reach the narrow concrete road by another waymark post. Turn LEFT. (For **Walk B** resume text in paragraph **3**.)

2 After a few yards take a narrow path angling away on the right. Soon take two right forks in quick succession to pass to the right of a limestone pavement. Follow the path along the limestone edge – *with a view down to the top of the former lighthouse*. Pass through a small rocky gully and fol-

3 Follow it down to Marine Drive. (*For refreshments turn right to the Rest & Be Thankful Café*). Go through a gateway opposite for good views of Great Orme's Head high cliffs, then follow the road past Ffynnon Gaseg (Mare's Well). As it bends left go through a gap by a gate. Angle LEFT to descend between limestone outcrops, then follow a path down the hillside to reach an old roadway. Keep ahead to a junction. Turn LEFT past a nearby enticing seat, then follow the old roadway past an information board to a gate. Go along Llys Helig Drive to rejoin Marine Drive. Go up the No Through road on the left, then down the waymarked right fork to Pen-y-Ffordd Goch. Continue with a path beside a wall then fence beneath the limestone crags, enjoying spectacular views, then rejoin Marine Drive.

9

WALK 7
AROUND THE GREAT ORME

DESCRIPTION A 5½ mile walk around this dramatic limestone headland, offering close views of its stunning cliff scenery and birdlife. The route first follows Marine Drive up to Pen-y-Gogarth (Great Orme's Head), with its vertical cliffs, former lighthouse and café. After a long steady descent, enjoying panoramic sea and mountain views, the route returns across the limestone hillside and through Haulfre Gardens (tea-rooms). Allow about 3 hours.
START Cenotaph, northern end of the North Shore Promenade, Llandudno [SH 782826].

*M**arine Drive** is a spectacular one-way toll road around the Great Orme which opened in 1878, to replace an 1858 path, which Prime Minister William Gladstone complained about during a visit in 1868. The Great Orme's scenery is best appreciated leisurely on foot from Marine Drive's pavement. You may see the famous feral Kashmir goats, said to originate from a pair sent with others from India as a present for Queen Victoria, which have been roaming wild here since the 1890s. The name 'Orme' is said to derive from a Viking name for 'sea monster' – an apt description when viewed from sea!*

I Go along the promenade, then follow the walkway behind the Grand Hotel (1901) to the iron pier (1876/7). Turn through its gated entrance then walk along the pavement overlooking the rocky shore past Happy Valley Gardens to reach the castellated toll house at the start of Marine Drive. Continue beneath the limestone cliffs at the eastern tip of the Great Orme – *a nesting site for seabirds and containing arches, formed by stone extraction. Shortly the road heads west, passes a side road, then rises steadily between limestone crags and steep cliffs – with a view ahead of the former Great Orme's Head lighthouse (1862-1985) – to eventually reach the Rest and Be Thankful Café. Shortly after passing Ffynnon Gaseg the road descends*

south-east – *offering extensive views to Anglesey and the Carneddau mountains.* Below is an area known as the Gunsite (See Walk 6 for more information). Eventually you reach another castellated toll house.

2 Go through a kissing gate near it, then follow the path ahead, soon bending up and continuing across the limestone hillside past seats. *Known as the Invalids or Lovers Walk, it has been a popular pathway since Victorian times, offering panoramic views across Llandudno.* After a gate continue through Haulfre Gardens, soon passing Haulfre Tea-rooms and toilets. Go down Cwlach Road and along the narrow road ahead to reach Old Road with its tram line. Follow it down to crossroads just below the Tram Station. *The cable tram to the summit opened in 1902/3.* Turn left along Church Walks and continue to the promenade.

WALK 8
LLANDUDNO TO CONWY

DESCRIPTION A 8½ mile highly scenic linear walk following a delightful section of the new Wales Coast Path from Llandudno to the medieval walled town of Conwy, returning (or starting) by regular bus [14,15 & 19 – a more limited service on Sundays]. From the North Shore the route follows spectacular Marine Drive around the Great Orme (cafe midway) to West Shore. It then follows the shoreline Conwy Estuary Trail to Deganwy and along the estuary edge, before crossing the river into Conwy. Allow about 5 hours. The route can easily be broken down into three shorter walks linked to bus services or extended to Conwy Nature Reserve (see Walk 11).
START Cenotaph, northern end of the North Shore Promenade, Llandudno [SH 782826].

*T**he stunning** medieval fortified walled town of Conwy standing near the mouth of the Afon Conwy estuary against a backdrop of mountains, is a designated World Heritage Site. Its impressive late 13thC castle*

The Great Orme

WALK 7

LLANDUDNO

① North Shore walk 23

Cenotaph

toll-house

Happy Valley

Pen-y-Gogarth

Cafe

former lighthouse

well

Marine Drive

boating lake

West Shore

cafe

Golf Course

WALK 8

A546

DEGANWY

station

Marina

Conwy

Deganwy Quay

Conwy Estuary

CONWY

A546

castle

station

link path to Conwy Nature Reserve

N

0 ¼ mile

was built for Edward I to strengthen his conquest of Wales, and the walls, over ¾ mile in length, originally with 22 towers enclosed a new town occupied by English settlers. Crossing the estuary are two historic bridges built by renowned engineers: Thomas Telford's graceful suspension bridge (1826) and the adjacent tubular railway bridge built by Robert Stephenson (1849). Conwy was once an important port and boats still continue the town's mussel fishing tradition. Today the estuary and marina are home to many small pleasure boats and yachts.

1 Follow instructions in paragraph **1** of **Walk 7**.

2 Continue along the pavement, then go along the promenade at West Shore past the boating lake – *with two small peaks ahead marking the site of Deganwy Castle (See Walk 10)*. After a car park, with a cafe nearby, continue along the wide shoreline Conwy Estuary Trail beneath dunes – *enjoying fine views across to Conwy mountain, along the coast to Penmaenmawr, and across to Anglesey*. Eventually you reach a shoreline road in Deganwy. *For centuries, until Telford's suspension bridge was opened in 1826, a ferry operated across the tidal river from here. A new river taxi service to Conwy began here in 2010*. At the railway crossing

go past the rear of toilets and continue with the estuary trail – *with a good view across to Conwy Marina*. After passing Deganwy Quay with its hidden marina the trail continues above the edge of the estuary – *enjoying good views to Conwy and its impressive castle*. Eventually the walkway splits at an information board just beyond the Conwy tunnel monument. (The left fork extends the recreational route to Conwy Nature Reserve.) Bear RIGHT to follow the lower of two pathways through gardens, then up to cross the bridge over the river to enter Conwy.

WALK 9

WEST SHORE

DESCRIPTION A simple but enjoyable 1½ mile walk featuring dunes, a shoreline walkway, and extensive views. Allow about 1 hour.

START Southern end of West Parade, West Shore, Llandudno [SH 774815].

DIRECTIONS West Parade is accessed from Llandudno centre or the A546 from Deganwy. At its southern end there is a car park and roadside parking.

I Go along Dale Road and at the junction turn RIGHT. Just after the road bends left, take a signposted path on the right. Follow it towards the large building, then through and along the top of dunes above the shoreline – *offering great views across to Anglesey, Conwy Mountain and the Carneddau mountains.* After passing through gorse keep with the waymarked path briefly along the edge of the golf course then descending to a shoreline walkway. Follow it RIGHT beneath the dunes and on back to the start.

WALK 10

DEGANWY CASTLE

DESCRIPTION A 5½ mile walk between Llandudno and Deganwy, featuring two sites of historical interest – an old watchtower and the ruins of Deganwy Castle, an excellent section of coast from the mouth of the Conwy estuary to West Shore in Llandudno, and extensive views. Allow about 3 hours.

START Southern end of West Parade, West Shore, Llandudno [SH 774815]. An alternative start can be made from Marine Drive, Deganwy [SH 776792] or a car park in Deganwy [SH 777798] – follow instructions from no. 4.

DIRECTIONS See **Walk 9**. To start in Deganwy either turn along Marine Crescent by the railway station and Deganwy Castle Hotel to find roadside shoreline parking, or continue north along the A546 to find a signposted car park along a road on the left. Cross the footbridge over the railway line to reach the shoreline route.

T he twin hills above Deganwy, known as Vardre, which have probably been occupied since Roman times, have witnessed centuries of settlement and warfare. During the 6th and 9thC, a castle built in 517 for Maelgwyn Gwynedd, occupied this site. In 1078, a new Norman castle was built here by Robert of Rhuddlan. During the 13thC Deganwy was a focus of the campaigns by the English Kings to exert control over Wales. In 1215, the castle was rebuilt by Llywelyn ap Iorwerth after successfully regaining land lost to King John, and after some years of peace, it withstood a siege by Henry III in 1245, but by 1257 was in English control. Walls and towers were constructed, encompassing both hills, but the castle was retaken and destroyed by Llywelyn ap Gruffyd (the Last) in 1263. When English control over Wales was finally established in 1284, Edward I decided to build a new castle across the river at Conwy. The few remains are largely those of Henry III's castle.

I Go along Dale Road and at the junction turn RIGHT, then follow the road (Trinity Crescent) to crossroads. Turn RIGHT and follow the main road past North Wales Golf Club and over the railway line, then turn LEFT up Hospital Road. After passing Maesdu Golf Club, turn RIGHT along Ffordd yr orsedd, then just before the entrance to Llandudno General Hospital, turn RIGHT along a side road and take the signposted path through a nearby kissing gate. Go along the edge of the golf course past the hospital, then cross a gap in a low shrub boundary and follow the path up rough pasture near the boundary. Shortly the path bends RIGHT to a footbridge and a ladder-stile. Go up the next field edge to cross a ladder-stile in the hedge/tree boundary ahead. Go up the field,

2 After about 40 yards bear RIGHT up the slope then continue beneath an area of gorse towards a telegraph pole to cross a waymarked ladder-stile by a gate. Go up to

LLANDUDNO

West Parade

West Shore

WALK 9

Golf Club

Hospital

N

0   ¼ mile

tower

Llanrhos

WALK 10

Castle ruins

DEGANWY

Station

A546

road. Go straight ahead along Hill View road, and at the T-junction turn RIGHT. Shortly, turn LEFT on a signposted path along the access lane to Maes Dalau farm/caravan park, soon bending right. Take the signposted path between a house and a long outbuilding to a stile and continue along a tree-lined path to a ladder-stile to enter the Vardre.

3 Keep ahead up the large field to cross a ladder-stile by a gate in the top fence corner. Just beyond turn RIGHT alongside the fence to cross a stile in the fence corner. (*The next section is courtesy of Mostyn Estates.*) Turn LEFT up along the fence towards the two small hills of Deganwy Castle. At sheep pens, angle RIGHT to go round the base of the first hill, then across an area of level ground to follow a path up the left-hand side of the second hill. *On its summit are the sparse ruins of the castle and panoramic views, including Deganwy and Conwy marinas, and Conwy castle.* Return down the path then turn LEFT and pass to the right of an isolated section of stonework. Now angle LEFT down to follow a path across the hill's northern slopes, with the castle walls visible above. About 20 yards from a fence and house ahead turn LEFT to follow a clear path through gorse and across the hill's bracken covered western slopes, then descend to a nearby small gate and follow the enclosed path to a road. Cross the road and follow it down to the A546 at Deganwy. Go along the signposted enclosed path opposite past the side of the Deganwy Castle Hotel. Cross a bridge over the railway, go through the alleyway ahead, and turn RIGHT along the road at the rear of houses, then LEFT to reach a road by the Conwy estuary – *with views to Conwy Castle and across to the marina.* Turn RIGHT.

the partially ruined tower ahead – *reputed to be one of a chain of coastal watchtowers built in the 17thC to warn of possible invaders or pirates. There are great views of Anglesey, the Great Orme, Llandudno, along the coast, and down the Conwy valley to the Carneddau mountains. Nearby are the twin hills of Deganwy Castle.* Return down the slope then turn RIGHT down the field edge to cross a ladder-stile in the fence. Angle LEFT down to another ladder-stile, then go across the next field to cross a further ladder-stile. Turn RIGHT and follow the stiled path along the edge of three fields to reach a road by St. Hilary's church at Llanrhos. Turn RIGHT, then soon turn RIGHT again along Cae Rhos. Go past houses and through a kissing gate ahead. Go along the field edge to another kissing gate, then follow the enclosed path between houses to emerge on a

4 Follow a delightful section of the new Wales Coast Path/North Wales Path along the promenade, then the wide shoreline recreational route beneath dunes towards the Great Orme to West Shore – *enjoying fine coastal and mountain views.*

13

WALK 11

CONWY RSPB NATURE RESERVE

DESCRIPTION A delightful almost 2 mile walk exploring the RSPB wetland Nature Reserve, with its Visitor Centre, shop and cafe, plus viewing screens and hides providing opportunities for watching birds on its two main lagoons. Created out of mud extracted during the building of the road tunnel under the Conwy estuary, the reserve now provides an important habitat for a variety of birds and other wildlife. The walk follows level wheelchair/pushchair friendly trail paths around the site later returning along the estuary with good views of mountains and Conwy Castle. Allow about 2 hours. (See available leaflet for shorter trails.) There is a small entrance charge for non-RSPB members, but this is well worth it.

START Visitor Centre, RSPB Nature Reserve [SH 797773].

DIRECTIONS The signposted reserve entrance is on the south side of the roundabout above the A55 at junction 18.

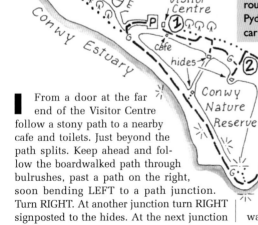

I From a door at the far end of the Visitor Centre follow a stony path to a nearby cafe and toilets. Just beyond the path splits. Keep ahead and follow the boardwalked path through bulrushes, past a path on the right, soon bending LEFT to a path junction. Turn RIGHT. At another junction turn RIGHT signposted to the hides. At the next junction

take the right fork to Tal-y-fan hide. Return to the junction and bear RIGHT, soon crossing a footbridge over a small pond and continuing to a wide cross path. First follow it RIGHT to Carneddau hide then return past your outward route.

2 At a stony track turn RIGHT. Follow it along the reserve's eastern edge to its southern tip by the estuary – *enjoying great views along the tidal river to the Carneddau mountains* – and round to gates. Just to you right is a viewing screen. Continue along the track past a vegetated area of the estuary – *a habitat for stoats* – and another viewing screen then nearby Benarth hide, to eventually reach the reserve's access road.

WALK 12

MARL HALL WOODS

DESCRIPTION A 1¼ mile walk around Marl Hall Woods, owned by Woodland Trust and offering free public access. The attractive ancient mature deciduous woodland, set on a small limestone hillside above Marle Hall, was once part of its extended garden. The route follows paths up around the edge of the wood to a breathtaking viewpoint. Allow about 1-1½ hours.

START Marl Hall Woods car park [SH 799787].

DIRECTIONS Leave the A55 at junction 19 and follow the A470 towards Llandudno. At a roundabout turn RIGHT signposted to Esgryn/ Pydew. Go past Esgryn Road to find the small car park on the right.

I Go through the kissing gate and follow the level wide stony path through the edge of the wood, soon passing behind Marle Hall. When the path splits continue on the lower left fork to cross a stone stile below an old well, where you are joined by a walled path. Turn RIGHT up the slope, then follow the stepped path by the wall – *known locally as Jacob's Ladder* – after which the path rises through the wood to a stile in a wall and an information board.

2 Here turn RIGHT up the woodland path. When it splits near the wall corner bend LEFT up the path to follow the wall along the edge of the wood past a path on the right, briefly descending and continuing by the wall – *with a glimpse of Bodysgallen Hall.* At the wall corner turn RIGHT and follow the wall to a stile at its end by a Welcome board – *with an obelisk on the skyline ahead.* Follow the path RIGHT up the wood edge.

3 At a fence corner where it levels out by a tree numbered B226 at a junction of paths, turn LEFT. Follow the path up the slope ahead and on along the wood edge near the fence, soon moving away and bending RIGHT. After a few yards take a path on the left through trees onto a small grassy shelf – *offering panoramic views from Conwy valley and castle to Anglesey – a great place to stop!* Go along the shelf for a few yards then turn RIGHT to rejoin the woodland path. Follow it north along the wood edge, soon descending to a path junction. Keep ahead, soon descending a stepped section of path and passing side paths. Soon after a path on the right the path bears LEFT down past another viewpoint across to Conwy castle to join your outward route near the wall corner. Descend to the information board, then turn LEFT down a path adjoining your outward path, soon bending left and passing under a crag, then angling down through the trees to join your lower outward route back to the car park.

WALK 13

BODYSGALLEN HALL

DESCRIPTION A 2½ mile woodland walk featuring a view of hidden historic Bodysgallen Hall. Allow about 1½ hours.
START As Walk 12.

*B*odysgallen Hall *is a restored mainly 17thC Grade I listed country house containing a late 13thC five storey tower, reputedly a watchtower for Conwy Castle. It has a long association with the wealthy Mostyn*

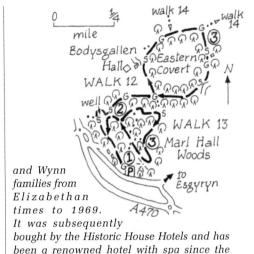

and Wynn families from Elizabethan times to 1969. It was subsequently bought by the Historic House Hotels and has been a renowned hotel with spa since the early 1980s. In 2008 the Company donated the property to the National Trust.

1 Follow instructions in paragraph **1** of **Walk 12**.

2 Cross the stile and follow the path through woodland to a kissing gate, then across the field – *with a glimpse of Bodysgallen Hall* – to a kissing gate onto a junction of paths. Turn LEFT and follow the narrow track beside Eastern Covert wood almost to its end at Bodysgallen Hall. Cross a stone stile on the right and follow the path ahead, soon angling away from the wall and descending, then continuing across the top of the field to a kissing gate/gate. Keep ahead. Go past a finger post and along the wood edge to a kissing gate at its corner.

3 Turn RIGHT briefly up alongside the wall then head up the field to a ladder-stile. Follow the path through young trees to a kissing gate, then follow the boundary on your left round to a stile by a gate in the wood corner. Just beyond follow a wide path through the wood down to join your outward route. After crossing the stile to re-enter Marl Hall Woods by the information board take the path ahead adjoining your outward path, soon bending left and passing under a crag, then angling down through the trees to rejoin your outward route.

WALK 14

GLODDAETH HALL

DESCRIPTION A 4½ mile walk (**A**) exploring an area of attractive part wooded countryside featuring two ancient country houses. The route follows good paths through Marl Hall Woods, Eastern Covert Wood and further woodland to visit the small community of Bryn Pydew. It then heads north through farmland, continues past Coed Isaf and the rear of Gloddaeth Hall, now St David's College, then returns by field paths to pass close by Bodysgallen Hall. Allow about 3 hours. The route can easily be shortened to a 2½ mile walk (**B**) or extended at the beginning or end by incorporating the circuit of Marl Hall Woods (see Walk 12).
START Marl Hall Woods car park [SH 799787].
DIRECTIONS Leave the A55 at junction 19 and follow the A470 towards Llandudno. At a roundabout turn RIGHT signposted to Esgryn/Pydew. Go past Esgryn Road to find a small car park on the right.

I Go through the kissing gate and follow the level wide stony path through the edge of the wood, soon passing behind Marle Hall. When the path splits continue on the lower left fork to cross a stone stile below an old well, where you are joined by a walled path. Turn RIGHT up the slope, then follow the stepped path by the wall – *known locally as Jacob's Ladder* – after which the path rises through the wood to a stile in a wall and an information board.

2 Cross the stile and follow the path through woodland to a kissing gate, then across the field to a kissing gate onto a junction of paths. Go along the path ahead signposted to the Obelisk up through Eastern Covert Wood. At the wood corner, just before a waymarked gap in the wall ahead and a gate, turn LEFT to cross a stile by a gate. Follow the right hand field edge round to a kissing gate/gate ahead. Follow the path through young trees to a ladder-stile. Angle

RIGHT down the field, later joining the boundary wall of the wood to reach a kissing gate in the bottom corner. Here turn RIGHT alongside the hedge and through a waymarked gateway ahead. (For **Walk B** continue beside the hedge down to a ladder-stile, then follow a farm track down the next field to a kissing gate/gate. Go along the hedge-lined green track to a kissing gate/gate on the left where it meets a more distinct track at point **6**.)

3 Angle RIGHT across the field to a stile into the wood. Follow the path up through the trees, shortly being joined by another, to pass a house. (An alternative, missing out Bryn Pydew, is to follow a narrow path on your left to a kissing gate and down through a wood to join the main route at a waymarked path junction by an old wall corner at point **4**. Turn left.) At an access road by Oaklands go along the lane ahead then at a gated entrance to a house turn RIGHT up a signposted enclosed path to pass behind the house. Keep ahead along the edge of an access track past the entrance to Highwinds, then follow the narrow waymarked path through three kissing gates to reach Bryn Pydew. Continue along the road then do a sharp U-turn LEFT along another road, passing beneath Ty Capel Bryn Pydew to cross a ladder-stile at an entrance to a driveway, Follow the waymarked path down the field edge, over a track and down to a kissing gate. The path continues down through trees to a waymarked path junction by an old wall corner. Take the path angling RIGHT.

4 Follow the waymarked enclosed path down the wood edge to a gate by a house. Go down its access track past outbuildings then cross a ladder-stile on the left. Now go along the edge of several fields (ladder-stiles) to a minor road, then follow it LEFT. At the junction cross the road to an iron kissing gate opposite. Go along an old green track, past the corner of Coed Isaf to a kissing gate. Follow the track along the edge of the wood. When it bends to a gate in the wall continue up the field/wood edge to a kissing gate, then up the field/wood edge to another kissing gate in the top corner. Follow the path alongside the large boundary wall of Gloddaeth Hall – *the former mansion of the Mostyn family, whose 16thC great hall, 17thC and later extensions now form part of St. David's College, an independent mixed day and boarding school which opened in 1965* – then go briefly along its access track. Go through a kissing gate on the left and follow the path along the field edge past a house.

5 At its garden corner angle LEFT to a kissing gate onto a driveway. Follow it LEFT past the house to a kissing gate opposite. Angle LEFT down the rough field to a stile in the bottom boundary and a kissing gate beyond. Go along the edge of the large field to a kissing gate just before the corner. Turn RIGHT along the green track to another kissing gate onto the road. Go along the farm track opposite to a kissing gate/ gate.

6 Follow the green track up the field to a stile/gate, then the edge of the next two fields to join a signposted cross path at Eastern Covert Wood. Turn RIGHT along the wood edge to a kissing gate, then follow a faint green track ahead along the top edge of the field. Just after it begins to bend right, angle up past a fenced tree to join a path near the wall above to cross a stone stile in its corner onto a track by nearby Bodysgallen Hall. (*See Walk 13 for information.*) Follow it LEFT beside the wood to rejoin your outward route. Follow it back to re-enter Marl Hall Woods by the information board. If energy allows turn left beside the wall to complete the woodland circuit (See Walk 12). If not go down the path ahead adjoining your outward path, soon bending left and passing under a crag, then angling down through the trees to re-join your outward route.

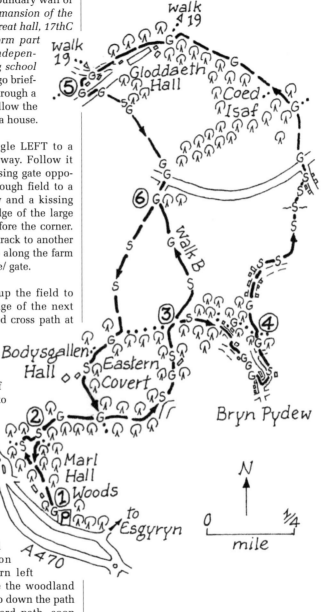

17

WALK 15

BRYN PYDEW

DESCRIPTION A 4½ mile walk (**A**) exploring the attractive undulating part wooded limestone countryside north west of Mochdre. From Bryn Pydew Nature Reserve the route follows paths to Glanwydden, with its country inn, then woodland and field paths to Bryn Pydew. After descending to the edge of Mochdre it returns up through the attractive conservation woodland of Coed Brongarth, owned by the Woodland Trust and crosses a small limestone ridge offering final panoramic views. Allow about 3 hours. The route can easily be shortened to a 3½ mile walk (**B**) by omitting Glanwydden.

START Car Park by Bryn Pydew Nature Reserve [SH 818798].

DIRECTIONS Follow the A547 east through Mochdre, past the Business Park then take a road on the left signposted Phoenix Workshops/ P. Follow the road to cross the A55. At the T-junction turn right signposted to Llangwstenin/ Glanwydden. Follow this minor road past a church, then go up its left fork, shortly levelling out to find a parking area on the right.

*B**ryn Pydew** Nature Reserve was created in 1976 by North Wales Wildlife Trust to protect its limestone pavement. From the northern end of the car park a path leads down to an information board, which outlines a suggested short circular route around the reserve.*

I Continue along the road to the entrance to Tan-y-Bryn Caravan Park. Here, turn RIGHT down an access lane to Wiga Farm Cottage. Follow a stony track to its end then continue along a limestone path. After passing an old limestone quarry – *whose stone was used to face houses in Llandudno* – the path bends sharp LEFT to a waymarked path junction. (For **Walk B** turn left and resume instructions in paragraph **3**.)

2 Turn RIGHT and follow the path to cottages, then go through a kissing gate on the right and another by a house. Follow the path along the edge of three fields then in

the corner of the third large field, turn LEFT along its edge and through a facing gate. Continue through two further fields, then between houses to the road at Glanwydden. (*For refreshments turn right to the nearby Queen's Head.*) Turn LEFT along the road to a kissing gate on the left beyond the last house. Follow the path up the field to an access lane. Turn LEFT to rejoin your outward route. Return along the path to the waymarked path junction at point **2**. Keep ahead.

3 At another waymarked path junction go up its left fork to a kissing gate. The path now rises steadily through a small wood to a kissing gate beneath a house, and continues to a kissing gate at the wood corner. Follow the enclosed path to another kissing gate, then continue ahead past a fence corner and on across a limestone exposed field to another kissing gate. Turn RIGHT down the road past houses, then cross a ladder-stile on the bend. Follow the meandering undulating path through a small wood. Just after passing a path on the right you reach a waymarked path junction at an old wall corner. Turn sharp LEFT up a path to a kissing gate. Continue up the sunken path, over a track by a gate and on up the field edge to a ladder-stile. Go along the initially rough lane into the small community of Bryn Pydew.

4 At crossroads go up the road ahead (Esgyryn/Llandudno Junction), shortly levelling out – *with good views* – then on the bend take a signposted path along an access track. It soon steadily descends to pass crags, then rises. Go past the track to Fron Heulog and continue down to Fron Farm. Go through a gate ahead and down a faint enclosed green track, then follow the hedge to a waymarked gateway. Continue ahead beside the boundary, soon on a steady descent towards Mochdre, to cross a stile/ footbridge in the field corner. Turn RIGHT down the field edge to a ladder-stile, then follow a stony track down to a road.

5 Follow it LEFT to a junction with Station Road. Keep ahead. At the signposted bridleway (Fford Bwgan) you have a choice. If you don't wish to visit Coed Brongarth simply follow the gated bridleway up its edge. Otherwise continue along the road past Five Gables to reach an access point into Coed Brongarth. Follow a wide path up the edge of the attractive woodland to reach an information board above a stile. Turn LEFT up the path, then go up another path on the right. At the top where it splits, follow the path LEFT up through the wood to a stile to join the bridleway. Follow it RIGHT along the wood edge to a green track by a waymarked gateway. Follow it RIGHT through trees to a stile/gate. Continue ahead on the green track, soon fading and bending up the hillside to cross the end of a small ridge near the top of the wood. Go on to another small grassy limestone ridge ahead – *offering extensive views* – then descend towards houses ahead, past a water trough and down to a small gate into Tan-y-Bryn Caravan Park. Follow its driveway ahead to the road. Turn RIGHT back to the start.

WALK 16
COED BRONGARTH

DESCRIPTION A short but rewarding undulating 2¼ mile walk featuring attractive woodland and extensive views. The route first heads to a limestone ridge, then descends through Coed Brongarth, an important conservation woodland owned by the Woodland Trust. It returns up a delightful adjoining bridleway and follows green tracks to Bryn Pydew, before a final short section of road walking. Allow about 1½ hours.
START As Walk 15.

Continue along the road, then go along the driveway to Tan-y-Bryn Caravan Park. After passing houses go through a small waymarked wooden gate ahead. Go up the slope to a water trough then continue up onto a grassy limestone ridge – *offering extensive views*. Go to the wood corner just below, then descend alongside the wood to cross a stile into Coed Brongarth. Follow the path down through the trees to a path junction, and continue ahead down to another. (Both junctions offer short cuts to the bridleway as shown.) Turn LEFT down to an information board, then follow a wide path RIGHT along the wood edge down to an exit to reach the road below.

2 Follow it RIGHT past Five Gables, then turn sharp RIGHT up the signposted bridleway (Fford Bwgan). Follow the delightful enclosed gated bridleway up the wood edge, past stiles. At a waymarked gateway turn LEFT up a green track, soon emerging into a field and levelling out. Continue ahead on another green track – *offering great views*. The track then descends steadily to a road by a sports ground at Bryn Pydew. Turn RIGHT and follow the attractive hedge-lined road back to the start.

WALK 17

MYNYDD PANT & NANT-Y-GAMAR

DESCRIPTION A 3¾ mile **(A)** or 3 mile **(B)** walk featuring a section of shoreline, two small limestone hills, attractive woodland, and panoramic views. Allow about 3 hours.
START Paddling pool/toilets/cafe, eastern end of North Shore promenade, Llandudno [SH 799822]. Roadside parking.

1 Walk east along the remainder of the promenade then the grassy foreshore towards the Little Orme. At Craigside join the pavement then cross the road and go up Ffynnon Sadwrn Lane opposite. *Ahead is the limestone hill of Mynydd Pant.* After passing Ffynnon Sadwrn well keep ahead on the signposted bridleway, then cross a ladder-stile on the right. Go along the edge of two fields to a road. Follow it LEFT then take a signposted bridleway up a lane on the right. Shortly follow the signposted bridleway through an iron gate on the left and through an area of limestone then gorse to a bridle gate and up to the bend of a road. Go up the road to its end at Pant Uchaf, then turn LEFT along a path to a small gate. Turn RIGHT along the narrow hedge-lined path, then up alongside the boundary.

2 A few yards beyond the boundary corner turn LEFT to follow a path through gorse and on up across the open limestone covered slope of Mynydd Pant, passing to the right of a large boulder – *a great place to stop to enjoy the panoramic coastal and mountain views.* Follow the path just below the gorse and limestone covered top and when the Little Orme comes into view ahead, as the land starts to descend, follow a path RIGHT through gorse – *with new views east along the coast to Rhyl and the Clwydian Range.* The path then bends up to the highest point with its grass-covered reservoir and masts. From the fence corner descend the wide limestone covered slope, soon heading down towards a large stone wall corner and passing through gorse. At the wall corner angle

RIGHT on a path down past a waymark post to a kissing gate into a wood. (For a shorter woodland walk follow the path ahead to exit the wood at point **3**.) For a fuller exploration of this delightful mature woodland, angle LEFT down a path to a small gate and continue down to a crossroad of paths. Here turn RIGHT up the path to a small gate. Follow the wide path ahead alongside the fence, soon descending. Pass to the right of a gate and continue along the wood edge. After about 20 yards the path bends RIGHT and rises steadily to exit the wood at a kissing gate.

3 Follow the path ahead beside the large wall to another kissing gate. Go up the path, then after about 10 yards angle away from the wall past a telegraph pole, continuing along a wide bridleway onto Nant-y-Gamar – *a SSSI with limestone grassland rich in a wide range of plant species.* At another telegraph pole, keep straight ahead up the limestone hillside to join a wide path – *with a good view across to Mynydd Pant and the Little Orme* – soon narrowing as it passes between gorse and bracken. You can continue with this path to a lane, but a better option is to follow a path on the right to the nearby highest point then on towards two white houses with the western side of the Great Orme and Anglesey beyond. Shortly the path descends to a gate in a hedge. Here follow another path LEFT alongside the hedge to a lane. Follow the lane to where it meets another. (For **Walk B** go ahead down to a kissing gate/cattle grid, then descend the narrow road. At crossroads follow the road ahead to North Shore.)

4 Turn LEFT between boulders by a gate to join a nearby access track, which you Follow past Tan-y-Coed cottage. At its end bear LEFT up a path and follow it to a superb viewpoint. Descend the waymarked zig-zag path – *offering panoramic views across Llandudno, west along the coast to Penmaenmawr, and along the Conwy Valley, with Conwy Castle visible* – then continue with the path across the steep slope beneath impressive limestone crags, soon descending. Just before a waymark post at a junction

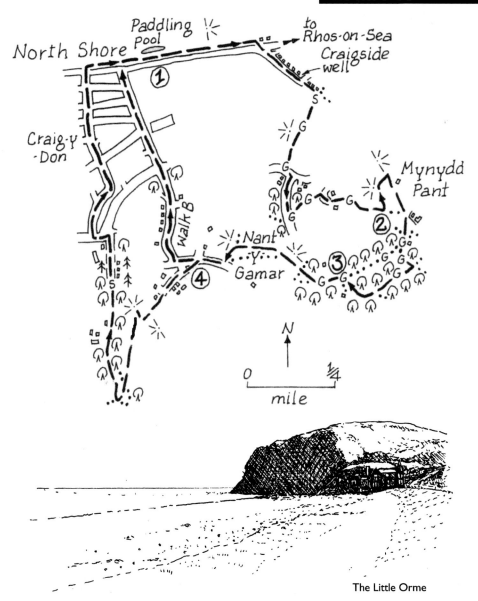

The Little Orme

of paths, take a path angling RIGHT down to a wall corner, where you join another path. Just before a kissing gate, turn RIGHT along a path beside a fence, soon descending to pass an old quarry and lime kiln, then a house. After a stone stile you reach Tan-y-Allt cottage. Follow its access track down to Fferm Bach Road in Craig-y-Don. Turn LEFT along the pavement opposite, then go down Roumania Crescent with its attractive large houses. Shortly take its right fork then follow Carmen Sylvia Road to North Shore. Go onto the promenade for a stroll back to the start and refreshments at the poolside café.

WALK 18

THE LITTLE ORME

DESCRIPTION A 2¼ mile walk exploring the Little Orme (463 feet/141 metres), a small limestone headland of great interest offering extensive views. Allow about 1½ hours. It can easily be combined with Walk 18.

START Penrhyn-side [SH 814818].

DIRECTIONS Follow the B5115 from Llandudno towards Penrhyn Bay, later rising past Craigside Manor/Premier Inn. Just before it descends to a dual carriageway, turn right into Bryn y Bia road to find a small parking area just beyond a bus shelter. Alternatively turn left along Pendre road to park by Penrhyn-side village hall.

The Little Orme is part of a line of limestone extending from Anglesey along the North Wales coast and south to Llangollen, formed from marine life over 320 million years ago when this area was a tropical sea. It is an area of short grassland, bare rock, cliff and woodland scrub, a Special Site of Scientific Interest, and includes Rhiwledyn Nature Reserve managed by the North Wales Wildlife Trust. It is home to a variety of sea and land birds, and contains many unusual plants. It has been a site of great archaeological importance since Neolithic times. In the 1580s, one of its caves housed a printing press, which secretly produced Catholic prayers, poetry and other manuscripts. Between 1889 to 1931, limestone was extensively quarried on the seaward side, from where it was shipped for use in blast furnaces in Scotland, and later in the manufacture of Portland cement. The site had its own narrow gauge railway and crushing plant. Between 1941-44, an artillery practice camp was based here, providing training in night firing.

1 Return to the B 5115 and follow it towards Llandudno. Cross the road and follow it to a kissing gate by an emergency telephone into Rhiwledyn Nature Reserve. Follow the waymarked North Wales Path (NWP) past an information board, after which it rises steadily. At a waymark post you can simply follow the NWP ahead up to a kissing gate. A more rewarding alternative is to take the left fork up the part limestone covered hillside to a small gate at a good viewpoint. Turn round then take a path angling LEFT up the slope, parallel with the nearby iron fence – *with new views to Rhos-on-Sea and beyond* – shortly descending near the fence to rejoin the NWP at an information board.

2 A few yards beyond the kissing gate, leave the NWP by turning LEFT and following a path briefly up alongside the tree boundary, through a gap in it, then on to pass an old wall corner. At another corner – *with a view across Llandudno Bay* – follow a path LEFT up to the summit trig point for superb all round views. Return down to point **2** then continue with the waymarked NWP across the gorse covered hillside, and down to a dramatic viewpoint overlooking the old quarry at the fence corner. Turn RIGHT and follow the waymarked path down to a stile at the top of an old incline near the concrete remains of a winding gantry. Go down the incline to a finger post.

3 A short diversion LEFT provides a good view of the cliffs with nesting birds and a small inlet. Return to the finger post then continue with the upgraded path past sections of iron fencing and on to an information board. Here leave the North Wales Path and continue along the wide stony path. When it splits, keep ahead to a hidden kissing gate, then go up a lane. Just beyond the second house, go through a kissing gate on the right. Follow the path through trees, keeping with the left fork up the wood edge, then the enclosed path to a farm. Follow its access lane to the B5115. Turn LEFT back to the start.

WALK 19

COED GAER

DESCRIPTION A 3 mile walk exploring attractive low limestone hills and woodland near Penrhyn-side, with panoramic views. Allow about 2 hours.
START Penrhyn-side village hall [SH 814816].
DIRECTIONS See Walk 18.

1 Return along Pendre road, then take a signposted stepped path on the left. Follow the enclosed path up to a road. Turn RIGHT, then LEFT to follow a track behind Mount Pleasant terrace, and on up to a good viewpoint. Cross a stile on the right and go up to a kissing gate. Angle LEFT through gorse then go up the limestone covered slope of Mynydd Pant to its summit with a small covered reservoir and masts to enjoy panoramic views. Return down the slope then head down towards a large wall corner, passing through gorse. Just before it, turn sharp RIGHT along a path to a waymarked gated fence corner. Follow the path beside the boundary, soon descending and becoming hedge-lined, to go through a small gate. Continue to a nearby access lane and follow it down. On the bend, take the signposted bridleway ahead down to a bridle gate, through gorse and down to an access track.

2 Go through the gate opposite and follow the path through the wood, soon keeping on its upper left fork and rising. At another path junction, angle LEFT up through trees to emerge onto the small limestone hill

of Nant-y-Gamar. Follow the path beside the hedge, then turn RIGHT along a lane. Where it meets another, turn LEFT through boulders by a gate and go along a track ahead past Tan-y-Coed. At the entrance to another house, with a garage ahead, turn LEFT up a path, which continues across open ground, soon rising to reach a stunning viewpoint. Follow the delightful waymarked path down the hillside, then across the steep slope beneath impressive limestone crags, soon descending steadily to a kissing gate in the wall corner near a house. Follow the path through the trees, then go up a track to a ladder-stile at the entrance to St David's College – *an independent school containing 16thC Gloddaeth Hall.* Continue beside its large boundary wall to a kissing gate into a field.

3 Follow the waymarked path directly ahead, rising steadily near the boundary of Coed Gaer to a kissing gate, then go up through the wood to another kissing gate into a field. Follow a path RIGHT near the wall to a kissing gate and on to another at the wall

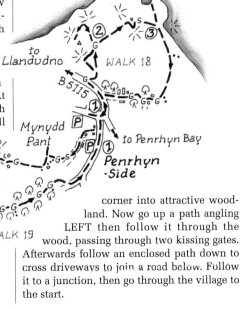

corner into attractive woodland. Now go up a path angling LEFT then follow it through the wood, passing through two kissing gates. Afterwards follow an enclosed path down to cross driveways to join a road below. Follow it to a junction, then go through the village to the start.

WALK 20

RHOS-ON-SEA

DESCRIPTION A 3½ mile walk exploring the small sea-side resort of Rhos-on-Sea, passing places of historical interest, including Llys Euryn, a ruined 15thC manor house, prominent 16thC Llandrillo Parish church and the tiny shoreline ancient St Trillo's Chapel. Allow about 2 hours. A Heritage Trail leaflet containing additional interesting information is available from the Tourist Information Point. The walk can easily be extended to include the waymarked trails on Bryn Euryn (See Walk 21).
START Clocktower/Tourist Information Point, Rhos-on-Sea promenade [SH 842805].

I Head along the promenade towards Colwyn pier – *enjoying views along the coast to Prestatyn.* At a snack bar at the edge of Rhos-on-Sea cross the coastal road and go up Cayley Promenade. *The unusual house on the corner of Bryn Mor road is the former home of eminent local mid 20thC architect Sidney Colwyn Foulkes, who designed several important buildings with his trademark stone pineapples.* Turn along Ebberston Road East. At a roundabout continue up Ebberston Road West opposite – *past the entrance to Heaton Place with its telltale pineapples* – to its end.

2 Turn RIGHT along Tan-y-Bryn road – *once an ancient trackway, possibly Roman. In late 19thC it became a prominent residential area for wealthy businessmen from Liverpool and Manchester who commuted daily by train. Only a few of the large Victorian houses, now Care Homes, remain.* Shortly you reach the entrance to Bryn Euryn Nature Reserve opposite Rhos Road. *For information on Bryn Euryn see Walk 21.* Go along its access road, then take the waymarked Summit Trail up steps on the right. Follow the path to an information board by the ruins of Llys Euryn. Continue with the waymarked trail, soon rising up the edge of woodland to a wide stony path by Llys Euryn Cottage. (From here you can follow either the Summit or Woodland Trails – see Walk 21.) Go through a nearby kissing gate then follow a choice of waymarked paths down to the car park. Continue along Tan-y-Bryn road to reach The Ship inn – *built in 1874.*

3 Turn LEFT along Llandudno Road, cross to the pavement opposite and continue to the 17thC lychgate of Llandrillo Church. *Standing on the hilltop site of an earlier 13th church, it dates mainly from the early 16thC. Its unusual shaped tower became part of a chain of coastal signal towers built in the 17thC to warn of pirates. The churchyard contains the grave of Harold Lowe – the heroic Titanic officer on the only lifeboat that returned to attempt to rescue drowning passengers.* Return along Llandudno Road, then turn LEFT down Church Road. Turn RIGHT along Elwy Road.

4 On its bend turn LEFT through a gateway into the park. Descend the path to pass between tennis courts and a children's playground. Turn RIGHT along Penrhyn Avenue, then LEFT up Colwyn Crescent. Continue ahead along Trillo Avenue, then cross Marine Drive. Turn LEFT , then take a path leading back to St Trillo's Chapel. *This tiny church stands on an ancient healing well, where the 6thC Celtic saint built his cell.* Continue along the promenade, soon joining Marine Drive. *Amongst the semi-circle of shops is the small former stone pier ticket office. Nothing remains of Rhos pier, which was bought second hand from Douglas in the Isle of Man at the end of the 19thC and erected here. From it there operated a regular passenger steamship service between Liverpool and Holyhead. It was demolished in 1954.* Continue past the small harbour – *created in the 1980s when the breakwater was built to prevent local flooding* – back to the start.

WALK 21

BRYN EURYN

DESCRIPTION A choice of two popular short waymarked trails exploring Bryn Euryn, a small part wooded limestone hill (430 feet/131 metres). Both trails visit the ruins of Llys Euryn. The 1 mile Summit Trail, with a few short steep climbs and descents, slippery after rain, extends to the hill's grassy top, with its ancient hillfort and panoramic views. The alternative 1½ mile Woodland Trail explores the hill's lower wooded slopes. Allow about 1½ hours.

START Bryn Euryn car park, Rhos-on-Sea [SH 834802].

DIRECTIONS The entrance lies at the western end of Rhos road.

Bryn Euryn is a Local Nature Reserve managed by Conwy Countryside Services. On its lower slopes are the remains of Llys Euryn – a 15thC fortified mansion built by Hugh Conwy, reputedly on the site of an earlier 13thC house owned by Ednyfed Fychan, chief advisor to Llewellyn the Great. Nearby is an old limestone quarry which opened in the 1840s. From here stone was taken by horse drawn railway down Rhos Road to a seafront jetty for shipping by boat. On its summit are the remains of a Romano-British hillfort and a World War II radar station.

| From the car park entrance follow the waymarked trail along the pavement, then up steps and on to an information board by the ruins of Llys Euryn. Continue with the waymarked trail up the edge of woodland to reach a wide stony path by Llys Euryn Cottage. Continue ahead along the stony path to where the trails split.

Summit Trail Follow the waymarked trail up through the wood, soon levelling out. Keep ahead through the trees to a crossroad of paths. Turn LEFT up through the trees then open hillside past seats to the trig point and information board on the top of Bryn Euryn. Follow the waymarked trail down the steep hillside towards the Little Orme and through trees to join your outward route. Return down the path to go through the kissing gate by Llys Euryn Cottage, then follow a choice of waymarked paths down to the car park.

Woodland Trail Follow the wide waymarked trail, soon briefly descending then passing side paths. Shortly the wide path rises steadily then at a waymarked side path it bends north. When it splits go up the narrower waymarked left fork, past a seat and on across the wooded slope. Shortly the trail descends through the trees then levels out. At a waymarked path junction, turn sharp RIGHT down the stony track to the car park.

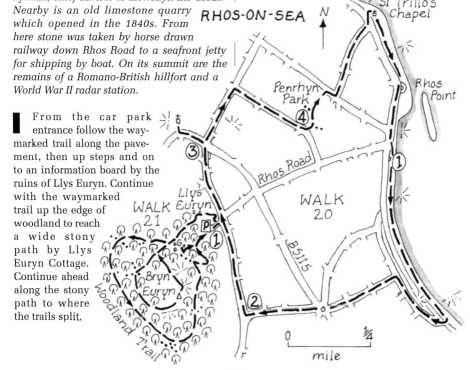

25

WALK 22

COED PWLLYCROCHAN

DESCRIPTION A 7¾ mile (**A**) walk, offering panoramic views, that meanders through the attractive undulating countryside bordering Mochdre, Colwyn Bay and Rhos-on-Sea, linking designated Countryside Sites. It visits Bryn Cadno Nature Reserve, the ancient woodland of Coed Pwllycrochan and the limestone hill of Bryn Euryn, a Nature Reserve and the site of an ancient hillfort. Allow about 4½ hours. The route includes alternative 6 mile (**B**), and 5 mile (**C**) walks using a link road past the Zoo (an optional visit).
START Mochdre [SH 826786].
DIRECTIONS Follow the A547 through Mochdre, and near a pelican crossing by shops, take a side road signposted Phoenix Workshops/ P to find a car park on the right.

I Cross the A547 and go along nearby Old Conway Road, then turn LEFT up Singleton Crescent. At a junction, turn LEFT and follow the road up the hillside. *This is the Old Highway, once part of a Roman road and later the Irish Mail coaching road from Chester to Holyhead. It runs past Colwyn Zoo and Coed Pwllycrochan, before descending to Abergele Road at Eirias Park.* After passing Seren-y-Dyffryn caravan park the road levels out. Cross a stile on the right by Thornhurst and follow the path to another stile. Go up the field. After about 100 yards, the path bears half-RIGHT up the slope, passes through gorse, then continues up near a fence to reach a superb viewpoint. Continue beside the fence, soon descending to a stile. After a second stile the path rises across appropriately named 'The View' to another stile, then continues through gorse to a kissing gate.

2 Go along the access track. (Shortly, for **Walk B**, cross a stile on the left and follow the waymarked path along the edge of four fields to join your outward route, then follow the road (Old Highway) east past

the zoo to rejoin the main walk at point **4**.) Follow the track then lane to reach Mynydd Lane. Follow it LEFT, and at a road junction, turn RIGHT. Take the second road on the left – Honeysuckle Lane. Just beyond Fir Tree cottage go through a kissing gate on the left to enter Bryn Cadno nature reserve. Follow the path across the hillside up to good viewpoint. Retrace your steps then continue up the lane. At its end follow a delightful tree-lined bridleway down to a road. Turn LEFT and follow this quiet country road down the edge of the attractive Nant y Groes valley, and up past Gwern-Tyno farm.

3 At the entrance to Fox Hill house, take the signposted path angling back up through the trees, and follow it through the edge of mature woodland. After a more open aspect go up the path's left fork to reach a stony access track. Go down the track then lane. Just before a junction is an information board on Coed Pwllycrochan. Here enter the wood and at the path junction just above turn LEFT and follow the path up through the trees. At a waymarked path junction, take the RIGHT fork. At a waymarked crossroad of paths follow the RIGHT fork across the wooded slope. Later descend to another information board by a road junction. Follow a path just above the road (Old Highway) to its bend by a stream, then along the wood edge above the road to the B5113 at crossroads. Go up the path opposite along the wood edge to another crossroads. Turn RIGHT. (For **Walk C**, go up Old Highway opposite, past the zoo, and on down to join your outward route.)

4 Follow Llanwrst Road down through junctions to the A547. Cross the road and the nearby footbridge over the A55 and railway line, then take a signposted path over a stile on the left. Follow the path along the bottom edge of the wood, soon rising alongside a fence to run parallel with the railway/A55. At a waymarked path junction do a sharp U-turn up to another waymarked path junction. Turn sharp LEFT up the woodland path, soon doing another sharp U-turn. At a waymarked path junction turn LEFT up through the attractive woodland. At another waymarked path junction keep ahead, then

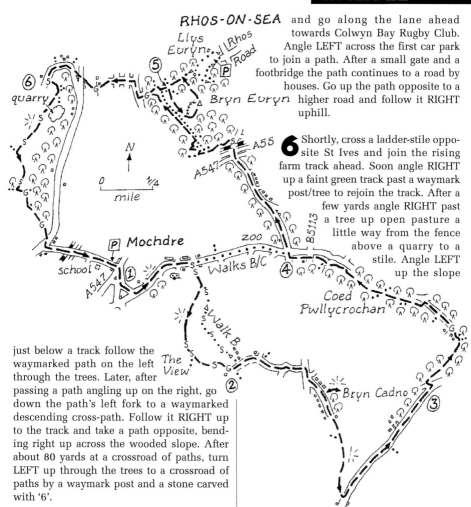

RHOS-ON-SEA and go along the lane ahead towards Colwyn Bay Rugby Club. Angle LEFT across the first car park to join a path. After a small gate and a footbridge the path continues to a road by houses. Go up the path opposite to a higher road and follow it RIGHT uphill.

6 Shortly, cross a ladder-stile opposite St Ives and join the rising farm track ahead. Soon angle RIGHT up a faint green track past a waymark post/tree to rejoin the track. After a few yards angle RIGHT past a tree up open pasture a little way from the fence above a quarry to a stile. Angle LEFT up the slope

just below a track follow the waymarked path on the left through the trees. Later, after passing a path angling up on the right, go down the path's left fork to a waymarked descending cross-path. Follow it RIGHT up to the track and take a path opposite, bending right up across the wooded slope. After about 80 yards at a crossroad of paths, turn LEFT up through the trees to a crossroad of paths by a waymark post and a stone carved with '6'.

5 Turn RIGHT and follow the waymarked Summit Trail up through the trees then open hillside past seats to the trig point and information board on the top of Bryn Euryn. Follow the waymarked Trail down the steep hillside towards the Little Orme and through trees to a wide cross-path. Follow it LEFT through the wood to join your outward route which you follow back down to the track. Take your outward path opposite down past the waymarked path junction to leave Bryn Euryn Nature Reserve by a kissing gate. Follow the lane to a nearby road. Turn RIGHT, then LEFT down Derwen Avenue,

ahead and continue along the broad ridge to a stile on a narrower limestone ridge ahead. Go along it, then after about 100 yards, bear LEFT up the stony end of another ridge and on down the field, soon bearing RIGHT to follow a faint green track to a stile/gate into a wood. Continue along the green track, then at an old waymarked gateway do a sharp U-turn LEFT down an enclosed bridleway. Go through a gate adjoining a stile giving access to Coed Cadw woodland, then continue down the delightful enclosed bridleway to the road. Turn RIGHT, then LEFT along Station Road back into Mochdre.

3 Go past its small harbour – *created in the 1980s when the breakwater was built to prevent local flooding* – then follow the lower cycle/walkway above the rocky shore to St Trillo's Chapel. *This tiny church stands on an ancient healing well, where the 6thC*

For Walk A continue along Abergele Road, then go down Beach Road. Shortly, cross a small bridge on the right over a stream. Continue beside the stream through Tan-y-Coed gardens to a road. *The gardens were created in the late 19thC by Sir Charles Woodall, a shipping magnate, who lived in a nearby mansion, now demolished. He built the castellated stone folly in 1894 as a retreat for smoking his pipe in the last years of his life!* Pass under the A55 and railway bridges to reach the promenade. Follow it west to the road leading up into Eirias Park at point **2**.

For Walk B follow the road through Eirias Park past the school to its end by the Leisure Centre. *The 47 acres of Eirias Park have provided leisure and recreation for the public since 1923. Its boating lake opened in 1935.* Follow a path down past the bowling green, then a road down to reach the promenade.

2 Head along the promenade towards Colwyn pier. *The pier opened in 1900 and was extended in 1903 to 750 feet long. The current pavilion was built in 1934 in Art Deco style. The pier has had a chequered history, with fire destroying two earlier pavilions, and is now in poor condition. After public support against its demolition there are hopes that funds can be found towards its eventual restoration.* Continue along the promenade to the Tourist Information Point and clock tower opposite the Cayley Arms in Rhos-on-Sea.

Celtic saint built his cell. Continue along the wide promenade. Shortly join the nearby road then continue on a raised walkway beside the sea-wall – *enjoying a good view to Llandrillo Church with Bryn Euryn beyond, and to the Carneddau mountains.* Go past the golf club – *where the first aeroplane landed in North Wales in 1910.* At the end of the sea-wall continue above the shore by iron railings.

4 About 30 yards before houses, descend steps on the waymarked North Wales Path and continue along the edge of the beach beneath gardens, then follow the NWP up steps then along a road through a housing estate. At its end go up steps to an information board on the Little Orme. (For **route b** turn left along the wide stony path. When it splits, keep ahead to a hidden kissing gate, then go up a lane. Just past the second house, go through a kissing gate on the right. Follow the path through trees, keeping with the left fork up the wood edge, then follow the enclosed path to a farm. Follow its access lane to the B5115. Turn right. to point **6**.)

5 For **route a** Turn RIGHT along the wide stony path to reach a finger post near an old quarry incline. Continue ahead for a good view of the cliffs with nesting birds and a small inlet, then return to follow the NWP up the incline to a stile at the top. Turn sharp LEFT and follow the waymarked path to a good viewpoint and up the hillside to join a fence. At its corner the path turns LEFT and rises through gorse. At a waymark post, where it levels out, ignore a path bending right but keep ahead to a kissing gate to enter Rhiwledyn Nature Reserve. Follow the path down to the road.

6 Go along the pavement towards the Great Orme, descending past Craigside Manor and Premier Inn. At the last house descend onto the grassy foreshore and continue to a paddling pool, cafe and toilets. Now simply follow the wide promenade along Llandudno's North Shore – *created along with the elegant buildings to provide a classical frontage to the new resort* – to the Cenotaph near its end.

WALK 23
OLD COLWYN TO LLANDUDNO

DESCRIPTION A 7¾ mile (**A**) or 7¼ mile (**B**) linear walk, offering extensive views, following a section of the Wales Coast Path/North Wales Path from Old Colwyn or Colwyn Bay to Llandudno, linked to frequent local bus services. After a short walk through Eirias Park or Tan y Coed gardens respectively the route heads along the promenade past Colwyn Pier to Rhos-on-Sea. After visiting the ancient St Trillo's Chapel it continues above the shore to Penrhyn Bay. After a short section of beach and a climb across the Little Orme (**route a**) or a lower alternative (**route b**) it descends to Craigside and follows the majestic promenade along Llandudno Bay. Allow about 4½ hours. The route can easily be undertaken as shorter walks linked to the same bus services.

START Abergele Road, Old Colwyn [SH 867783] or Eirias Park entrance, Colwyn Bay [SH 856782].

DIRECTIONS First take the no. 12 (Rhyl) 14 or 15 (Llysfaen) bus from stop D in Mostyn Street, Llandudno centre to Colwyn Bay. Alight at Eirias Park for Walk B or The Royal College of Nursing building opposite The Plough in Abergele Road, Old Colwyn for Walk A.

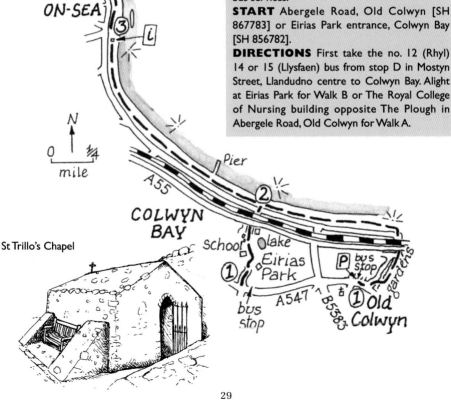

St Trillo's Chapel

29

WALK 24

MYNYDD MARIAN

DESCRIPTION A 7¼ mile (**A**) or 6 mile (**B**) walk that combines an interesting section of coastline between Llanddulas and Old Colwyn, with attractive limestone countryside, incorporating sections of the North Wales Path (NWP). After a section of the popular Wales Coast Path the route heads inland via the wooded Fairy Glen up to Mynydd Marian nature reserve, featuring an early 19thC telegraph station and offering extensive views. Walk A returns beneath impressive Craig y Forwyn and through an attractive wooded valley. Walk B returns from Llysfaen via road. Allow about 4 hours.

START Shoreline car park, Llanddulas [SH 907786].

DIRECTIONS Leave the A55 for Llanddulas and follow signs for the beach to reach the parking area and toilets.

I Follow the cycle/walkway west along the shoreline towards Colwyn Bay, later passing two conveyor belt carrying jetties. *For centuries, limestone from the nearby Llanddulas/Llysfaen quarries has been transported by sea from here. In the 18thC, small single masted flat bottomed barges were beached and loaded from horse drawn carts. In the 19thC, wooden jetties were built to accommodate sailing sloops, and later the famous Gem line of steamers, which operated until the 1930s. Before the introduction of conveyor belts which enabled stone to be moved directly from the quarry to ships, loading was provided by teams of men, working to the tide. Nowadays, ships up to 4,000 tons berth alongside the second 660 foot jetty, arriving 3 hours before high tide and leaving within 1 hour of high tide occurring.* Continue past a small rocky headland. Just before a road turn LEFT under the railway and A55 bridges. Cross the road to a path opposite signposted to Fairy Glen/Min-y-don. Continue beside the stream through Tan-y-Coed gardens – *created in the late 19thC by Sir Charles Woodall, a shipping magnate, who lived in a nearby mansion, now demolished. He also built the castellated stone folly which he used as a retreat for smoking his pipe!*

2 Continue through an underpass at Old Colwyn. Keep ahead alongside the stream past houses, then go up a stepped path to roads above. Turn RIGHT along Fairy Glen past houses, then follow a pathway ahead down into Fairy Glen Local Nature Reserve. Just before a footbridge, follow a path LEFT through the attractive narrow wooded valley past side paths to a road. Cross the road and turn RIGHT. Soon, turn LEFT on the NWP between houses, then angle RIGHT up the golf course to a gate in the corner onto a road. Go along the track opposite to a stile/gate ahead. Turn LEFT up the edge of the field and golf course to a stile, then turn LEFT up a hedge-lined track.

3 At a gate and signposted path junction you leave the NWP by continuing up the track signposted to Marian Bach. When it levels out turn LEFT past a small rock face and continue along a fading green track. At the boundary ahead follow it RIGHT up through two fields. Cross a track then turn RIGHT up a tree/hedge lined path to a stile. Just beyond, bear LEFT to follow an old wall to cross a ladder-stile. Go past the end of two large corrugated barns, then along the second barn's side. Keep ahead past Ty Mawr's complex of buildings then at houses go down a concrete track on the left past outbuildings to a signposted path junction. Follow a path RIGHT , then the driveway to the road. Turn RIGHT and soon do a sharp U-turn LEFT past Anneddle bungalow and follow the track past houses. At Rose Villa, turn sharp RIGHT up a track, then pass between boulders to enter Mynydd Marian Reserve. Follow the path

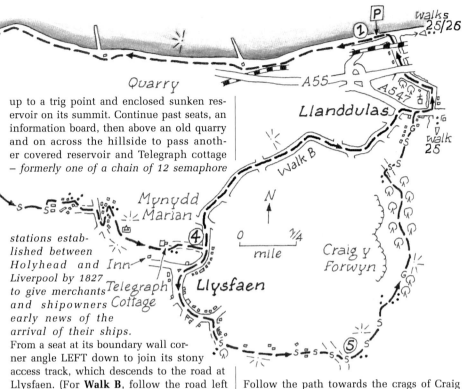

up to a trig point and enclosed sunken reservoir on its summit. Continue past seats, an information board, then above an old quarry and on across the hillside to pass another covered reservoir and Telegraph cottage – *formerly one of a chain of 12 semaphore*

stations established between Holyhead and Liverpool by 1827 to give merchants and shipowners early news of the arrival of their ships. From a seat at its boundary wall corner angle LEFT down to join its stony access track, which descends to the road at Llysfaen. (For **Walk B**, follow the road left down into Llanddulas.)

4 Follow it RIGHT through the village, then at a junction, angle LEFT down to another road. Follow it past a converted chapel and at the junction keep straight ahead. At another junction keep ahead. Just beyond the bend take the signposted NWP on the right along an access lane then track. Just past the entrance to Bryn Celyn, cross a stile up on your left. Follow the wall along the limestone ridge. At its corner, keep ahead across the hillside past a bungalow, then beneath a small caravan site to cross a stile. Follow the path to pass between two buildings and on to a stile. After another stile, turn RIGHT along a track to cross a ladder-stile.

5 Go along a green track. After about 50 yards, angle LEFT, soon rising to follow the wall ahead round to a stile. Just beyond turn RIGHT then follow a path up the slope and across the rough terrain to a ladder-stile.

Follow the path towards the crags of Craig y Forwyn (Maiden's Leap) – *with its tales of a local girl's spurned love and suicide.* After about 50 yards, keep ahead up its right fork, then after another 20 yards, follow another path RIGHT across a small limestone ridge. Soon the path begins a steady descent through bracken, then beneath Craig y Forwyn's scree slopes to an iron gate. After another short descent the path levels out and continues through the attractive wooded valley to eventually reach a minor road. Cross the stile opposite and follow the path down to a stile. Go along the left-hand field edge to a stile/gate and down the next field past houses to a kissing gate. Go down the short access lane, then enclosed path to the road by the Valentine Inn. Cross the road and turn RIGHT past St Cynbryd's church, then LEFT along Beach Road. It soon crosses the river and continues past Dolydd picnic area to a junction. Turn RIGHT under the A55 road bridge and continue beside the river. Go under the railway bridge, then follow the

CWM DULAS & GOPA WOOD

DESCRIPTION A 7 mile walk of great variety exploring the coast and unspoilt rural hinterland between Abergele and Llanddulas, featuring two hillforts sites and good views. The route starts with a 2¼ mile section of the Wales Coast Path (WCP) to Llanddulas, then heads inland up the hidden attractive Dulas valley. It passes beneath Pen-y-corddyn-mawr, with an option to visit its hillfort. It then heads across fields to Gopa Wood, an attractive wooded hill managed by the Woodland Trust, with an opportunity to visit to hidden Castell Cawr fort. Allow about 4 hours.
START Pensarn beach [SH 942786]
DIRECTIONS From Pensarn on the A548 coast road go over the railway by the station, and follow it to the third car park by the promenade just beyond the Beach Café.

*P*en-y-corddyn-mawr *hillfort stands on a impressive limestone hill overlooking the Dulas valley, an Open Access area, about a mile south of Llandulas, and near the Roman road to Caerhun in the Conwy valley. The large fort's defences consist of natural steep cliffs on three sides and two stone ramparts and ditches on its northern side. Although dating from early Iron Age the finding of various Roman artefacts indicates its use extended into the Roman period, with speculation that it may have been the site of a Roman healing shrine.*

Walk west along the promenade then join the nearby coastal cycle/walkway. (For an alternative initial section follow a stony path above Pensarn's pebble beach.) *Inland, amongst the densely wooded hillside, stands the picturesque but sadly ruined Gwrych Castle. The gothic castellated mansion, with its towers and walls, was built in 1819-22 for Lloyd Bamford Hesketh.* The WCP then runs close by the shoreline, passes the Tides café bistro and caravan park, then Llanddulas honeycomb worm reef – *a rare and newly formed coastal feature visible at low tide.* It joins the Afon Dulas where it enters the sea, soon crossing a bridge over the river.

2 Just before a road bear LEFT along an embanked path beside the river under

the railway bridge. Go under the A55 road bridge, then turn LEFT along Beach road. It passes Dolydd riverside picnic area, crosses the river and continues to the main road in Llanddulas. Turn LEFT then RIGHT along Beaulah Avenue past the stylish village hall. Go past sides roads opposite an attractive converted 19th C church and continue down Bryn Dulas road. After crossing the river the road rises to a small junction by Bryn Dulas Farm then continues south along Cwm Dulas, passing beneath the densely wooded slopes of Craig y Forwyn – *with a good view ahead of Pen-y-corddyn-mawr.* When it splits at the outskirts of Llysfaen go down Cwymp road, past a side road, over the river, and past the attractive Cwymp Mill. Continue up the road.

3 On the next bend, turn RIGHT on the signposted path along an access track to the gated entrance to Country View. The delightful path continues through trees to a stile, then rises across the wooded slope, shortly passing beneath houses to a kissing

Pensarn Beach

o caravan park

gate onto a road beyond at Rhyd-y-foel. Turn LEFT, then cross a stile on the right opposite Shire Cottage. Follow the meandering path up through the wood to emerge from the trees by the fence beneath Pen-y-corddyn-mawr's impressive limestone crags. From here a path rises across the slope. After about 40 yards go up its left fork to join a wider path just above, which rises steadily across the gorse-covered scree slopes – *enjoying a good view across the valley to the limestone escarpment of Craig y Forwyn (Maiden's Leap) and the mountains of Snowdonia.* After levelling out the path continues along the left-hand

Golf Club

Castell Cawr

Gopa Wood

Betws Lodge Wood

edge of an area of gorse to join the fence descending from Pen-y-corddyn-mawr. Just before its corner the fence is low enough to allow access to the hill's south-western slopes to visit the hillfort, with a small pile of stones at its highest point. Then at the fence corner go through a gap in the old tree boundary and follow a path through the narrow field to cross the old boundary at its end by a small ruin. Descend the slope to another path below. Follow it down to a stile and old gate.

4 Continue down the path then near the fence on your right beneath Pen-y-corddyn-mawr's wooded slope to pass behind houses to a stile/gate by an outbuilding onto the driveway below. Turn RIGHT towards Garth Gogof then LEFT across the

toilets

P café

station to A548 Rhyl

A55

A547

ABERGELE

Park yard and through a gate at the end of an outbuilding. Follow the stiled path through three fields, then half-RIGHT down the next to a lane. Cross the stile opposite and go along the field edge to gates, then up to the corner of Betws Lodge Wood. Follow the gated track along the edge of two fields past the wood to a large barn. Angle LEFT to a gate and follow a track past Tyddyn-uchaf farm, then another track ahead.

5 On its bend cross a stile ahead into Gopa Wood. Go up the path to a green track, and follow it LEFT, then take an initially wide path angling RIGHT through the trees. Soon divert RIGHT along a side path to the impressive ramparts of Castell Cawr hillfort. Return to continue north through the wood. At a cliff edge warning post the path bends down to cross a nearby footbridge over Ffos y Bleiddiaid – *a deep narrow cleft mined for lead and copper, possibly since Roman times.* The path continues through the wood, soon descending steadily to a track. (*For a splendid viewpoint turn left to the nearby bend.*) Turn RIGHT down the track, soon doing a sharp U-turn at a good viewpoint. Just before it bends left, descend a long stepped path on your right to a road junction on the edge of Abergele. Go down Tan-y-Gopa road, past the golf club, then turn LEFT along Ffordd Tan'r Allt to the A547 by the entrance to Gwrych Castle. Follow it RIGHT towards Abergele centre, then cross it to go along Sea Road opposite, shortly passing the park and crossing the A55 and railway line to reach the start.

WALK 26
PENSARN TO OLD COLWYN

DESCRIPTION A 5 mile linear walk, linked to a regular local bus service, following a section of the Wales Coast Path/beach from Pensarn to Old Colwyn, offering fine coastal views and plenty of interest. From the promenade the hard surfaced cycle/walkway heads west. At Llandulas it passes a rare honeycomb worm reef, accessible at low tide, then continues past two conveyor belt carrying jetties linked to a nearby limestone quarry. Later the route heads inland through Tan-y-Coed gardens to the main road in Old Colwyn, from where frequent no. 12 buses will return you to Pensarn. Allow about 2½ hours. The route is covered on maps for Walks 24 and 25.
START Promenade near Abergele and Pensarn railway station [SH 946787]. Plenty of free parking is available.

I Follow instructions in paragraph **1** of Walk 25 to Llandulas. At a road continue ahead along the cycle/walkway passing toilets and a parking area. Now follow instructions in paragraph **1** of Walk 24. Then at the end of Tan-y-Coed gardens cross over the stream and go up Beach Road to the main road in Old Colwyn. A bus stop is along the road to the right opposite The Plough.

WALK 27
RHYL TO PENSARN

DESCRIPTION A 4½ mile linear walk linked to a regular local bus services (or train) following the Wales Coast Path/ North Wales Path along the designated cycle/walkway from Rhyl to Pensarn beach by Abergele & Pensarn railway station. Plenty of free parking is available by Pensarn beach. From the nearby main road opposite Slaters there are frequent no. 12 buses to Rhyl. Allow about 2½ hours.
START Rhyl centre/bus station [SJ 009813]

Rhyl developed from a small village at the beginning of the 19th C into a fashionable elegant Victorian seaside resort with visitors arriving by regular steamer services from Liverpool, then later the railway. The small Forydd harbour grew in importance due to the demise of the port at Rhuddlan as a result of the silting of the river Clwyd and the development of the holiday resort. In the 19thC the harbour boasted a boatyard and a fleet of fishing boats. Now crossing the harbour is Pont y Ddraig, an elegant lift bridge for pedestrians and cyclists, part of a major redevelopment in 2013 to this historic part of Rhyl.

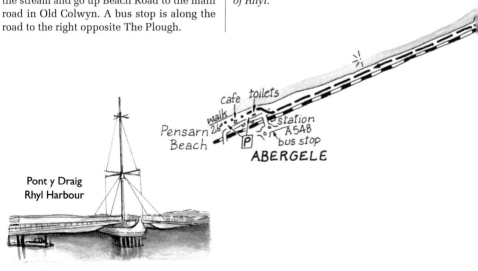

Pont y Draig
Rhyl Harbour

1 Go along Rhyl's main shopping street to the clock tower roundabout and on to reach the nearby Seaquarium. Head west along the promenade above the extensive beach at low tide, soon passing behind the cinema and skytower – *enjoying a good view of the coast extending to the Little Orme, with the mountains of Snowdonia, beyond.* Later you continue beside the road to reach Foryd harbour, where the river Clwyd joins the sea. After crossing Pont y Ddraig you have a choice: Go past the end of the nearby Harbour Hub, with its popular cafe, then follow the wide cycle/walkway ahead alongside the boat park perimeter fence to the shore. For an alternative Wales Coast Path route just beyond do a U-turn back towards the bridge, then turn sharp LEFT to follow a choice of boardwalked paths up to a viewing platform, with information boards, on Horton's Nose – *the remains of once extensive dunes.* Continue down to join the cycle/walkway.

2 The Wales Coast Path continues west past a caravan site, Kimnel Dunes - a Local Nature Reserve - car park and further dunes. After Golden Sands Holiday Park walk along a raised railed path by the boulder sea defence, then continue beside the railway line, later passing above Pensarn shingle beach – *with Grwych castle prominent ahead* – then the beach car park to reach the road and promenade by Abergele & Pensarn railway station.

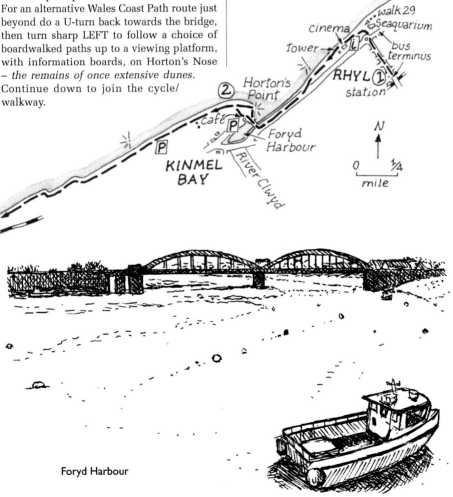

Foryd Harbour

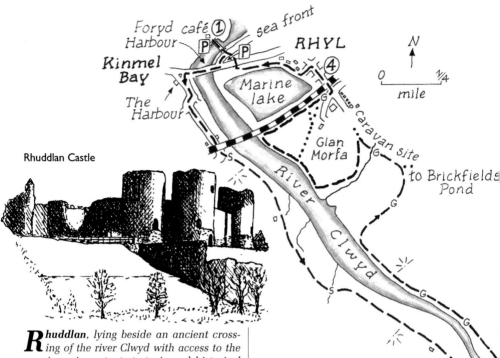

Foryd café ① sea front
Harbour
P
P
RHYL ④
Kinmel Bay
Marine lake
The Harbour
Glan Morfa
caravan site
to Brickfields Pond
River Clwyd
N
0 ¼ mile

Rhuddlan Castle

*R*huddlan, lying beside an ancient cross-ing of the river Clwyd with access to the sea, is an important strategic and historical site. It was a key gateway offering the easi-est access into the heartland of North Wales and for centuries was the focus of struggles between the Welsh and English. A motte and bailey castle was built in 1073 on Twt (look-out) Hill, reputedly on the site of an ear-lier Welsh stronghold. Nearby was a ditched Norman town, with its own priory. In 1277, Edward 1 chose an alternative site for a new castle, completed in 1281 - the first of sev-eral concentric castles he had built in North Wales - to reinforce his conquest campaigns. An impressive piece of medieval engineer-ing was the conversion of the river into a deep water channel to facilitate improved seaborne access. A new town, which still forms the heart of Rhuddlan was built at the same time. In 1284, after the power of the Welsh had been broken, Edward held a Parliament at Rhuddlan, which set out the constitutional settlement for Wales in the 'statute of Rhuddlan'. In 1646, the castle was dismantled after being captured by General Mytton and the Parliamentarians. Rhuddlan remained an important port serving the Vale of Clwyd, with a quay built below the church.

However, silting of the river and the develop-ment of Foryd harbour during the growth of Rhyl as a Victorian seaside resort led to its eventual demise.

Cross the Pont y Draig over the harbour and turn RIGHT to a crossing point to the right of a roundabout. Continue along the pavement opposite to cross the Foryd Bridge over the river. This bridge (1880) prevent-ed masted ships from reaching Rhuddlan, but the river port continued to export tim-ber, grain and lead ore, despite the develop-ment of Foryd harbour. Turn LEFT along Old Foryd Road. The road passes through a small housing estate and becomes Clwyd Bank. After passing under the railway line, turn LEFT on a signposted path to a stile and con-tinue along the western flood embankment of the estuary – with Rhuddlan castle promi-nent in the distance. Later a track runs along-side the embankment. Eventually, at caravan parks, continue along Marsh Road, passing under the A525 and by the small retail park (refreshment options) to the main road opposite the entrance to Rhuddlan Nature Reserve. Follow it LEFT to cross the footbridge over the river alongside the ancient stone road bridge. (To return directly to Rhyl turn left, following instructions in paragraph 3.) Go up the road into Rhuddlan.

2 Turn RIGHT along Castle Street to reach Rhuddlan Castle. After visiting the castle, continue along Hylas Lane. After about 75 yards take an enclosed path on the right by Castle Hill. After a kissing gate continue ahead to visit the distinctive mound of Twt Hill – *occupying a commanding position above the river.* Afterwards rejoin the main path which continues near the hedge perimeter of a caravan park, then bears LEFT to a stile/ gate onto a road. Follow it LEFT past the caravan park entrance and houses, then turn LEFT along Hylas Lane. Follow it past the school entrance and a thatched cottage back to the castle entrance. Go along Castle Street to the High Street, then down to the bridges over the river.

CLWYD ESTUARY & RHUDDLAN

DESCRIPTION A 7½ mile walk that combines a circuit of the tidal Clwyd estuary - a birdwatcher's paradise (binoculars highly recommended) – with a visit to Rhuddlan's places of historical interest – a Norman fortress site, its massive 13thC stone castle, and medieval church. It starts from Rhyl's redeveloped harbour featuring an elegant lift bridge and one of my favourite cafés. Allow about 4 hours. It can easily be undertaken as two separate walks of 1 and 6½ miles and started from Rhuddlan. For information on Rhyl see Walk 27.

START Harbour Hub, Rhyl [SH 995808]

DIRECTIONS After crossing the Blue Foryd Bridge over the mouth of the river Clwyd from Rhyl into Kimnel Bay turn right along Horton's Nose Lane, by the Mayquay pub, to the Harbour Hub, with car park.

peaceful backwater, home to a great variety of birds. According to tradition, it is also the site of battle in 795, when Caradoc, Prince of Gwynedd, and many supporters, were killed in battle by Offa, King of Mercia. Later, the gated cycle/walkway route bends away from the river, then passes a signed route to Brickfields Pond and continues past a caravan site to a junction at an information board on Glan Morfa Nature Reserve. Here turn LEFT along the edge of Glan Morfa, past Marsh Tracks, Rhyl's cycling centre, soon rejoining the estuary, which you follow towards the railway bridge, before bending away to leave Glan Morfa at a kissing gate.

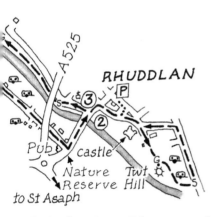

3 Go along Tan-yr-Eglwys to pass beneath St Mary's – *originally a single naved church founded about 1300 to serve the new town, but later a second nave and tower were added.* At a junction bear LEFT to join a tarmaced cycle/walkway/NCR 84. Follow it under the Rhuddlan by-pass and along the flood embankment close by the river Clwyd. *After centuries of sea-going vessels passing along the estuary it is now a*

4 Go across the footbridge over the railway line and along a road. At the second set of crossroads, turn LEFT to reach the Marine Lake, with its boating and miniature railway. Go along the edge of the lake, past the miniature railway's Central Station, then cross the railway line to a nearby road. Cross it then turn RIGHT and continue round the car park perimeter to cross another road and nearby Pont y Draig to the Harbour Hub.

WALK 29

PRESTATYN TO RHYL

DESCRIPTION A 4½ mile walk incorporating a section of the Wales Coast Path from Prestatyn promenade to Rhyl, linked to local bus services. This level walkway/cycleway features sand dunes, extensive beaches and great coastal views. Allow about 2 hours. The route is described from Prestatyn centre/bus station, but you may prefer to start from the promenade by the Nova Centre, using plentiful available parking. For information on Rhyl see Walk 27.

START Prestatyn centre/bus station [SJ 065829]

1 From Prestatyn bus station adjoining the town centre follow the road over the railway line to traffic lights on the A458 coast road. Go along Bastion Road opposite, following signs for Nova Centre/Beaches. On the bend by the Nova Centre go up a pathway ahead past Café Cymru to reach Dechrau a diwedd (beginning and end), the large Sun sculpture beyond marking the start/finish of the Offa's Dyke Path.

2 From the Sun sculpture head west along the promenade above the beach – now on the Wales Coast Path, passing behind the Nova Centre, past a car park, then sand dunes. *Ahead lies Rhyl, and the coast extending to the Little Orme, with the distant mountains of Snowdonia visible on a clear day. Out to sea are windfarms.* Continue along the top of a sloping sea defence. The shared recreational route continues along the promenade past the golf course to Rhyl, where you join the wide attractive Rhyl promenade above the expansive beach at low tide. *The beach contains many groynes to prevent sand erosion by the sea.* Continue past the Pavilion Theatre and Lifeboat station. Just beyond the Seaquarium turn left up a roadway, then bear left to the nearby bus terminus for a choice of buses back to Prestatyn.

Rhyl Promenade

WALK 30

GRONANT DUNES

DESCRIPTION A 3 mile walk following the Wales Coast Path through Gronant Dunes, a designated Local Nature Reserve and Special Site of Scientific Interest, returning through Prestatyn Golf Course, whose clubhouse offers refreshments to non-members. Allow about 1½ hours. The dunes, extending east from a single narrow ridge into a series of parallel ridges, support a range of insects and plants, including the dominant marram grass, and less common species such as sea-holly, pyramidal orchid, sea and portland spurge. The foreshore and shingle attract a variety of birds, including wintering waders, cormorants and the largest breeding colony of little terns in Wales.

START Barkby Beach car park, Prestatyn [SJ 068840]

DIRECTIONS On the eastern outskirts of Prestatyn, turn off the A548 coast road along Barkby Avenue, signposted to Barkby beach. Go past Pontins, and on the bend enter the beach car park by Prestatyn Sailing Club.

1 From the end of the car park follow the signposted Wales Coast Path (low tide route/Gronant) along a short section of promenade then a sandy path by Gronant Dunes above the rocky foreshore. Go up a fenced wooden walkway to an information board on top of the dunes, where you are joined by the alternative high tide route. Follow the initially boardwalked WCP east along the top of the dunes. The well waymarked WCP then bends briefly left and continues along the edge then through the middle of the expansive dunes – *with the distant former Point of Ayr lighthouse visible ahead* – later becoming more enclosed. Visible on the nearby hills above Gronant is the white house of Foel Nant – *the former Voelnant Telegraph station, dating from 1841*. After ¾ mile at a finger post turn LEFT along a boardwalked path across the dunes to a viewing platform overlooking Gronant Beach – *providing an opportunity to observe the little tern colony (do not disturb) and enjoy coastal views.* Return to the finger post then continue on the WCP signposted to Presthaven to pass along the edge of a small shallow reedy lake (dry sometimes).

2 Midway, the WCP turns inland and continues across Prestatyn Gutter to a tarmaced cycle/walkway. Follow it RIGHT near the attractive Prestatyn Gutter through Prestatyn Golf Course to the Clubhouse. Continue along its driveway then a road past bungalows. At the junction turn right on the cycle/walkway alongside Barkby Avenue, over Prestatyn Gutter and past Pontins to the start.

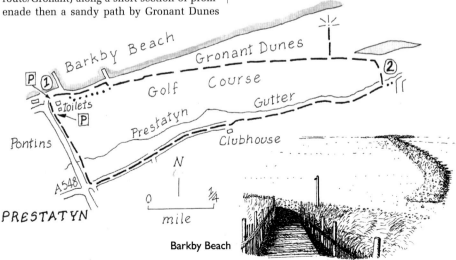

Barkby Beach

PRONUNCIATION

Welsh	English equivalent
c	always hard, as in **c**at
ch	as in the Scottish word lo**ch**
dd	as th in **th**en
f	as f in o**f**
ff	as ff in o**ff**
g	always hard as in **g**ot
ll	no real equivalent. It is like 'th' in then, but with an 'L' sound added to it, giving 'thlan' for the pronunciation of the Welsh 'Llan'.

In Welsh the accent usually falls on the last-but-one syllable of a word.

KEY TO THE MAPS

- ➡ Walk route and direction
- ═══ Metalled road
- ━ ━ ━ Unsurfaced road
- •••• Footpath/route adjoining walk route
- ∿→ River/stream
- ⚘ ♧ Trees
- ▄▆▄ Railway
- **G** Gate
- **S** Stile
- F.B. Footbridge
- ⋎ Viewpoint
- Ⓟ Parking
- Ⓣ Telephone

About the author, David Berry

David is an experienced walker with a love of the countryside and an interest in local history. He is the author of a series of walks guidebooks covering North Wales, where he has lived and worked for many years, as well as a freelance writer for Walking Wales magazine. He has worked as a Rights of Way surveyor across North Wales and served as a member of Denbighshire Local Access Forum.

Whether on a riverside ramble, mountain or long distance walk, he greatly appreciates the beauty, culture and history of the landscape and hopes that his comprehensive guidebooks will encourage people to explore on foot its diverse scenery and rich heritage.

Visit: www.davidberrywalks.co.uk

THE COUNTRYSIDE CODE

- Be safe – plan ahead and follow any signs
- Leave gates and property as you find them
- Protect plants and animals, and take your litter home
- Keep dogs under close control
- Consider other people

Open Access
Some routes cross areas of land where walkers have the legal right of access under The CRoW Act 2000 introduced in May 2005. Access can be subject to restrictions and closure for land management or safety reasons for up to 28 days a year. Details from: www.naturalresourceswales.gov.uk. Please respect any notices.

Problems with paths/Rights of Way Contact Conwy County Borough Council Countryside Service and Rights of Way Section (01492 574000 or via www.conwy.gov. uk) regarding any problems encountered in its area.

Public transport information Conwy County Borough Council produce a comprehensive information booklet on local bus and train services covering this area east to Rhyl. Contact Bws Conwy (01492 575562 or email: bwsconwy@conwy.gov.uk
Contact Denbighshire County Council for bus timetables between Rhyl and Prestatyn (01824 706968; www. denbighshire.gov.uk/transport)
Traveline Cymru: 0871 200 2233

Published by **Kittiwake-Books Limited**
3 Glantwymyn Village Workshops, Glantwymyn, Machynlleth, Montgomeryshire SY20 8LY
© Text & map research: David Berry 2011
© Maps & illustrations: Kittiwake 2011
Drawings by Morag Perrott
Cover photos: Main – Llandudno Pier to the Little Orme.
Inset – The Great Orme Tramway. David Berry

Care has been taken to be accurate. However neither the author nor the publisher can accept responsibility for any errors which may appear, or their consequences. If you are in any doubt about access, check before you proceed.

Printed by Mixam UK.

ISBN: **978 1 902302 91 1**